The Truth abou

An Islander's Memoir

REV. DONALD JOHN GILLIES

EDITED BY

John Randall

BIRLINN

First published in Great Britain in 2010 by
John Donald, an imprint of Birlinn Ltd

West Newington House
10 Newington Road
Edinburgh
EH9 1QS

www.birlinn.co.uk

ISBN: 978 1 780272 08 5

Reprinted in 2010
This edition reprinted in 2014 by Birlinn Ltd

The publishers gratefully acknowledge
the support of the Scotland Inheritance Fund
towards the publication of this book

British Library Cataloguing-in-Publication Data
A catalogue record for this book is available
on request from the British Library

Typeset by Antony Gray
Printed and bound in Italy by Grafica Veneta

Contents

Foreword Harry McGrath — vii

Editor's Introduction — xi

Brief Chronology for Rev. Donald John Gillies — xxv

THE NOTEBOOKS — 1

Select Bibliography — 163

Foreword

In 2003 the Centre for Scottish Studies at Simon Fraser University started to collect and archive material related to the history of the Scots in British Columbia. The project appealed immediately to the Scottish community. I soon found myself rooting through the dusty recesses of the Scottish Cultural Centre in Vancouver, recovering photographs associated with the long and storied history of piping in the province. Later, I combed the minute books of various Sons of Scotland camps in British Columbia, and examined one of the few remaining copies of a souvenir booklet produced by the United Council of Scottish Societies in 1928 to commemorate Ramsay MacDonald's unveiling of the Burns Statue in Vancouver's Stanley Park.

The Scottish community in British Columbia was, and is, very close-knit, and many of the collected items were brought to my attention through a chain of association. Such was the case with the memoirs of Reverend Donald John Gillies. The process of discovery stretched back to St Kilda itself and visits made there between 2001 and 2003 by my friend Professor James Russell of the University of British Columbia. These visits stimulated Professor Russell's interest in the archipelago and its former inhabitants and, back in Vancouver, he started giving lectures on St Kilda.

In late 2003, James Russell attended a concert organised by the Gaelic Society of Vancouver and a Mrs McIver, originally from the Island of Lewis, told him of Reverend Donald John Gillies. Reverend Gillies, she explained, was a widely admired Gaelic Presbyterian minister, who was born and raised on St Kilda before migrating to Canada. He died in Vancouver in 1993. James mentioned Reverend Gillies at a subsequent lecture on St Kilda and was gratified to find Lew Ross in the audience. Lew is a personal friend of Reverend Gillies's daughter Peggy Askew and it was he who made the initial contact with Peggy and reported that 'we had struck gold' for our archive project.

Soon thereafter James Russell and I found ourselves sitting in Peggy Askew's house in Coquitlam, British Columbia, enjoying her hospitality and going through seven 'jotters' filled with the stories of her father's long life. Peggy later told me that she remembered her father sitting at the dining room table over several winter months in the mid 1980s (when the Reverend Gillies was in his eighties) and 'writing his memories of St Kilda'. He seemed, she said, 'very committed to the job at hand'. On first reading the journals, I could sense this commitment – the author wringing memories from a tiring mind; his handwriting tailing off towards the end of a long shift and the story taken up again after a break, often with a pen of a different colour: blue followed by black followed by green. James soon turned the contents of the notebooks into a particularly diverting lecture and brought Reverend Gillies's words to life for local audiences. I was fortunate enough to hear him deliver such a lecture at Brock House in Vancouver, a few months after we visited Peggy.

I left Vancouver in 2007 and returned to live in Scotland. Peggy gave me permission to take her father's notebooks with me. We hoped that they could be made available through preservation and publication to the ever-growing army of scholars, writers and members of the public with an interest in the history and culture of St Kilda.

In November 2008, through the good offices of Curator Maria Castrillo, the notebooks were acquired by the National Library of Scotland. An extract from one of them was later used in a major NLS exhibition entitled 'The Original Export: Stories of Scottish Emigration'. Finally, in May 2009, Mairi Sutherland of Birlinn publishers in Edinburgh wrote to inform me that a grant had been acquired from The Scotland Inheritance Fund and that the Gillies memoirs were to be prepared for publication.

My thanks go to Neville Moir of Birlinn for recognising the

value of the Gillies notebooks when they were first shown to him and to Mairi Sutherland for the hard work and perseverance that led eventually to their publication. Thank you also to John Randall. His vast knowledge of St Kilda is most impressive and his sensitive editing of the journals much appreciated.

In British Columbia thanks are due to Professor James Russell for initiating the entire enterprise and for the generous help and advice he provided to me from my first viewing the memoirs in 2004 through to their publication in 2010. Thank you to Lew Ross without whose intercession the connection to Peggy Askew may never have been made and to Professor Ian Ross for the letter he wrote testifying to the importance of the memoirs and urging their publication. Above all, thank you to Peggy Askew (née Gillies) and her husband Don for their patience, kindness and support during a long but, I hope, ultimately satisfying process.

Harry McGrath
Chairman of Cultural Connect Scotland.
Former Co-ordinator of the Centre for Scottish Studies at Simon Fraser University, British Columbia, Canada.

Editor's Introduction

Writings about St Kilda

Such is the worldwide fascination with St Kilda that over 700 books or articles have been written about it (see the bibliography in 'Revised Nomination of St Kilda for inclusion in the World Heritage Site List', Scottish Executive, 2003). This is a remarkable and possibly unique quantity of writing about one small group of islands. Moreover, the flood of publications shows no sign of drying up – rather the contrary.

Perhaps even more remarkable is that, with just a small handful of exceptions, almost all this writing has been by outsiders rather than by native St Kildans, and almost all in English rather than in Gaelic, the language of the St Kildans. Many of the books have been written by people who have only set foot on St Kilda for a short time, if at all, and many have repeated uncritically views or apparent facts set out by previous authors.

It is possible to see a process of myth-making at work. As I have argued elsewhere, myths may of course contain elements of truth, but tend to be over-simplifications of reality and frequently owe their survival to the fact that they appeal to the popular imagination (*St Kilda – Myth and Reality*, The Islands Book Trust, 2007). From at least the time of Martin Martin, whose 'Late Voyage to St Kilda' was first published in 1698, ideas and theories about life on St Kilda have been promoted (sometimes consciously in pursuit of political or other agendas) which have shaped the pre-conceptions of subsequent visitors and writers.

For example, a pervading notion (which may be called the 'Myth of the Noble Savage' – see *St Kilda – Myth and Reality*) is that, prior to its corruption and undermining by the outside world, St Kildans lived an idyllic life in harmony with nature and other members of their small self-contained community. The following quotation from Martin Martin has echoed through the centuries: 'The inhabitants of St Kilda are much happier than the generality of Mankind, being almost the only People in the World who feel the Sweetness of true Liberty. What the Condition of the People in the Golden Age is feigned by the Poets to be, that theirs really is, I mean, in Innocency and Simplicity, Purity, mutual Love and cordial Friendship, free from solicitous Cares, and anxious Covetousness; from Envy, Deceit and Dissimulation; from Ambition and Pride, and the Consequences which attend them.'

Other myths about St Kilda are more recent in origin. For example, as shown by Michael Robson in his meticulously researched *St Kilda: Church, Visitors and 'Natives'* (2005), popular conceptions of the St Kilda 'Parliament', the St Kilda 'mail-boat', and indeed the role played in St Kilda in the second half of the nineteenth century by the Free Church of Scotland and particularly the Rev. John Mackay, owe much to the personal interests and eye for a good story of the journalist John Sands ('Out of this World; or, Life in St Kilda', 1876 and 1878). The conventional wisdom has become that the part played by religion, particularly in the nineteenth century, was a contributory factor if not a leading cause of the plight of the islanders, which eventually caused them to give up the struggle for survival and request evacuation (*The Life and Death of St Kilda*, Steel, 1965).

Now is not the time to enter into a detailed discussion of the various myths about St Kilda, how they have come about, and what relationship they bear to factual evidence. The key point is that the historiography of St Kilda consists mainly of writings from the outside, often with little first-hand knowledge of the subject under discussion, sometimes with a clear political or religious agenda, and frequently doing little more than repeating the conventional wisdoms of previous writing. In such circumstances, it is hardly surprising that myths are created and perpetuated.

In passing, we may contrast this situation with that of the Great

Blasket Island off the Dingle peninsula in County Kerry, Ireland. The Blasket islands, evacuated in the 1950s, in some ways occupy a rather similar iconic status in Irish history to that of St Kilda in Scotland. But there is one huge difference. Our knowledge of life on the Great Blasket comes not only from the outside, but from a whole library of books written by the islanders themselves, many in Irish Gaelic: for example, by Tomas O'Crohan, Maurice O'Sullivan, and Peig Sayers. The reasons for this contrast merit deeper study, since they seem to reflect not only the obvious differences of religion, but more importantly the very different ways in which the culture of the Great Blasket and St Kilda were regarded, and valued (or not), by the respective Governments and societies of the two countries prior to the evacuations.

It is against this background that the significance of the present volume can be seen: the memoirs of the Rev. Donald John Gillies, who was born on St Kilda in 1901 and left the island in 1924, emigrating to Canada to pursue his missionary calling in 1927. Also included are some memories by his elder brother, Neil, who was born in 1896, and left the island in 1919, but returned regularly during the summers of the years 1931 to 1939 following the evacuation in 1930 to look after the island for the new proprietor, Lord Dumfries. There are descriptions of Neil Gillies during his spells on the island as 'watcher' at this time in other books (see *Island Going*, Robert Atkinson, 1949).

These are some of the few accounts of life on St Kilda from the inside, by native St Kildans, albeit written in English – as is the other comparable autobiographical account by Calum MacDonald (1908–1979), extensive extracts from which have already appeared in David Quine's *St Kilda Portraits* (1988) and which is to be published in its entirety by The Islands Book Trust in 2010. Also of note are the memoirs of Calum or Malcolm MacQueen (1828–1913), one of the St Kildans who emigrated to Australia in 1852, as dictated to his son in Australia and published in part by both David Quine and Calum Ferguson, and by the Scottish Genealogy Society (1995). Calum Fergusson's *Hiort – Far na laigh a'ghrian*

(1995) is remarkable for being written in Gaelic, although not by a native-born St Kildan, and contains many St Kildan songs and stories. A selection of St Kildan songs has been recorded by Anne Lorne Gillies. However, it is inevitably difficult to be certain how far some of the songs and stories, even where it seems clear that they were first composed by St Kildans, may have been amended over the years by others.

The Family of Donald John Gillies and his brother Neil

Details of the ancestry of Neil (1896–1989) and Donald John Gillies (1901–1993) are given in Bill Lawson's *Croft History – Isle of St Kilda* (1993). Some of their other brothers (for example, Donald) are mentioned in the manuscript. They were the sons of John Gillies (1861–1926) and his second wife Ann Ferguson (1865–1952) of Croft No 15 Hiort, situated close to the west end of the village street, at a distance from the church and school.

The Gillieses occupied this croft ever since the new village and crofts were laid out in 1836, replacing the former settlement to the north of the graveyard and the previous run-rig system. Neil and Donald John's great-grandfather, John Gillies, is recorded in the first unofficial census of St Kilda taken by the Rev. John MacDonald of Ferintosh ('The Apostle of the North') in 1822. It would appear that the Gillieses were one of the families from Skye which re-populated St Kilda after an epidemic of smallpox almost wiped out the community in about 1727. On their mother's side, Neil and Donald John were descended from the Fergusons of Crofts Nos 4 and 5 Hiort, whose ancestors moved to St Kilda from Berneray in Harris after 1727.

Through both sides of the family, the brothers were related to individuals who played an important part in the history of St Kilda. One of their great-grandfather's brothers was the colourful and much-travelled Ewen Gillies, who emigrated to Australia in 1852, and then returned to St Kilda to re-marry before emigrating again (to Canada) in 1889. One of their mother's brothers was Neil Ferguson, the St Kilda postmaster, and their mother was descended from both Donald and Neil Ferguson, elders who had played a prominent part in previous disputes with the Free Church Minister and catechist on the island. So there can be no doubt that Neil and Donald John came from families at the centre of St Kildan life, and are therefore well-placed to give accounts of island life from the inside.

The Manuscript

The circumstances of the discovery of Donald John Gillies's manuscript in Vancouver, after his death in 1994, are outlined in the contribution by Harry McGrath. Clearly, we owe a great debt to Harry McGrath and Jim Russell, and also to John Donald publishers for undertaking the present publication.

The accounts included in this volume are edited versions of the original manuscript written in long hand in seven notebooks by the Rev. Donald John Gillies. The notebooks used were standard school exercise books (entitled Hi Class, by Hilroy, made in Western Canada) consisting of blank sheets of paper with 8mm wide ruled lines. The notebooks are numbered 1–7, and have brief notes on the cover indicating what they contain, but otherwise the narrative flows from one notebook to the next without any clear break.

Indeed, there is little attempt made by the author to structure the memoirs, just a few section headings but no chapter headings. Moreover, the text moves in an apparently unplanned way from subject area to subject area, frequently digressing and repeating itself, and shifting erratically from one time period to another. The narrative appears to be interspersed with extracts from newspaper articles from time to time, although these are not clearly identified as different from the author's own observations. Even the distinction between Donald John's memoir and what appears to be a section by or about Neil in the first part of notebook 7, but written in the same hand-writing as the rest of the manuscript, is unclear; and it has been necessary to make assumptions about the authorship. A section in notebook 7 apparently recording an interview between Neil and a Mr Hamilton on the island in the 1930s shortly after the evacuation is particularly confusing.

In editing the manuscript, a 'light hand' has been used in order to preserve as much as possible of the original style while correcting definite errors of grammar, spelling and punctuation. The guiding principle has been to try to make the flow of words intelligible to the reader, breaking undifferentiated text into sentences, inserting some extra section headings (which have been marked as such), and introducing punctuation where this is necessary to make clear the meaning. The names of ships and Gaelic words have been set in italics, to conform with usual style. Without these amendments, much of the text would frequently be difficult or impossible to decipher.

Nonetheless, the text remains largely in the form written down. It contains some incomplete sentences, repetition, and examples of what to a contemporary eye would be regarded as unusual construction and composition. Unusual spellings of place-names (for example Connacher and Stac Birroch or Birrock, instead of the more normal Conachair and Stac Biorach) and proper names (for example SS *Dunra Castle* instead of SS *Dunara Castle*) have normally been retained since these may be of interest. Donald Gillies's use of 'St Kildians' (rather than 'St Kildans' in more common use today) has been kept throughout. Other stylistic points, such as his references to 'the wife', and the attachment of the term 'Scotland' to most place-names on the Scottish mainland, have also been retained.

It seems at first sight strange that a Minister like the Rev. Donald John Gillies should write in this way. It should be borne in mind, however, that he was in his mid 80s when he was writing much of the memoir and this may account for some of the repetition and loose style. Part of the explanation may also be that he is a native Gaelic speaker writing in an acquired language. Certainly, there are spelling errors which can be attributed to this, for example, the fairly systematic rendering of 'contended' for 'contented'. More generally, sentence construction often tends to reflect Gaelic ordering and styles of speech. But the issue goes deeper than this. It is difficult to escape the conclusion that Donald John Gillies, while no doubt a fluent speaker and preacher, was uncomfortable when attempting to commit his thoughts to paper, whether in Gaelic or English. So even Gaelic words are sometimes recorded phonetically rather than as written, for example 'sho' for 'seo' (meaning 'this'). It is perhaps easier to interpret the manuscript as an attempt by someone brought up in an overwhelmingly oral culture to write down his thoughts in an unfamiliar medium. The challenges faced by Gaelic-speaking islanders who may lack the confidence to write in Gaelic, and write down in English exactly as they speak in Gaelic, with Gaelic idioms unconsciously interwoven, has been described by Donald Meek (2007).

The centrality of oral culture to Donald John's upbringing, as to life on St Kilda more generally, may also help to explain the rambling and repetitive written style, and the frequent diversions in the narrative. So what starts out as a description of a drowning or a fall from the cliffs is side-tracked into an account of the family history or character of the people concerned, even if this information may already have been provided several times before. Just as oral story-tellers rely on frequently repeated motifs or phrases to stimulate the memory, so particular facts associated with a person or place are rehearsed whenever the name is mentioned, for example the Rev John MacDonald's initial landing at Glen Bay on the north side of Hiort rather than Village Bay because of the weather conditions. There are also some discrepancies over dates, which have been left as in the original.

Insights into St Kildan Life

But despite these idiosyncracies, the manuscript is of great interest, often absorbingly so. Its value lies in the rarity of first-hand accounts of life on the island from the inside, rather than the observations of visitors. A few fundamental points can be selected.

Perhaps first and foremost is the overwhelming importance and pervasiveness of religion to life on St Kilda. Even allowing for the fact that Donald John Gillies became a Minister and could therefore perhaps be seen as unrepresentative, there can be no escaping the central role which Presbyterian religion, and the view of the world which it embodied, played in St Kildan life. From the very first pages of the narrative to the last, there is no doubt that the purpose of life, and the values which are to be treasured and upheld, derive from Christianity and the teachings of the Bible. Donald John's mother only read religious books and had an unwavering faith in the truth of the Bible. Donald John's father, like other prominent members of the community, had a deep knowledge of the Bible. The standing of men depended to a considerable extent on their ability to quote from and interpret the Bible, for example on *La Ceist* at the communions. A large number of the stories told by the St Kildans seem to have been derived from the Bible, or have biblical allusions, to which Donald John draws attention.

And there is no suggestion that this was in any sense a dogma forced on the people by dominant Ministers or elders, as some of the popular caricatures of St Kildan life would suggest. On the contrary, religion was the vital integrating force of community life, apparently accepted and wholeheartedly endorsed by the great majority of St Kildans. Christianity was at the heart of their culture, a culture worthy of respect and acclaim rather than criticism and ridicule, as Professor Donald Meek has pointed out in the sermon he preached at Greyfriars and Highland Tolbooth Kirk in Edinburgh in August 2009. Family worship was central to daily life. Sundays were observed universally and unquestioningly as the Lord's Day. The values of humility, love and kindness, and the need for salvation, were celebrated and accepted. In all of this, it is doubtful whether St Kildans were so different from many other rural Gaelic-speaking communities at that time in the Presbyterian parts of the Outer Hebrides. Outside observers, many of whom had never visited other places in the Hebrides, saw St Kilda as a place apart when in many ways its customs and beliefs were typical of a much wider area.

A further fascinating and important point is Donald John's analysis of the reasons for St Kilda's decline and eventual abandonment. In his view, and those of others whom he spoke to after the evacuation in 1930, the basic reason was lack of manpower to carry out community tasks, a gradually worsening predicament which he traces to the impact of the First World War. The stationing of military forces and installations on the island during the First World War led to a greater understanding by many of the younger generation of St Kildans of the perceived benefits of life outside the island. Once a few families and younger people migrated, it became progressively more difficult for the community to sustain itself.

Nor was this decline and eventual evacuation seen by most of the St Kildans as a source of regret. While there was inevitably and understandably nostalgia for the old days, and certainly a feeling that many valuable things had been lost, it is striking that all those interviewed by Donald John and his brother on the mainland following the evacuation were of the view that the move had been inevitable and indeed on balance beneficial. Apart from criticism that the Government had failed for many years to supply a postal service to the island, there seems to have been no resentment at the community's treatment by the authorities – indeed at several points Donald John is at pains to emphasise how well the St Kildans were treated both before and at the time of the evacuation.

Beyond these general conclusions, the manuscript sheds invaluable light on many day to day or year to year customs and beliefs. For example, the periodic excursions of men to Boreray to see to the sheep and cut peats is outlined in a matter-of-fact and unsentimental way which adds to our understanding of the economic functions which Boreray (and also Soay and Dun) played in St Kildan life. The various underground dwellings on Boreray, each belonging to a particular family, are described, along with the system of sending messages from Boreray to Hirta involving the cutting of turf patches at particular spots on Boreray visible from the main island. And the role of the St Kildan Parliament, sensationalised and exaggerated by the journalist John Sands in the

1870s, is clarified. It did not meet on a daily basis, and its key role during Donald John's childhood was to decide on the allocation of birds and bird-cliffs between the various families on the island. Like the role of the Church, one doubts whether the Parliament was so different from gatherings in many other islands or rural areas where communal activity of one sort or another was vital to the economic functioning of the community.

And intriguingly, Donald John at one point regrets that no writer had visited St Kilda, as John Millington Synge had visited the Aran islands (and others had visited the Blasket islands) in Ireland to record the history and stories of the island before it was too late. While one wonders how far this was a view original to Donald John, this was indeed a tragedy, because it appears clear that it was the influence of outside scholars and writers which stimulated the native people of the Blasket islands to write down their own memories. That nothing of this kind happened on St Kilda ultimately reflects the fact that the culture of St Kilda was not valued by the outside world before it was too late. Far from being seen as a source of cultural inspiration, the St Kildans were widely regarded as a curious and anachronistic phenomenon by both journalists and tourists from an assumed superior society, to be patronised or ridiculed rather than valued. As a result, we have no native St Kildan 'Library' of writings, merely fragments of songs and memories, and a very few longer accounts of life on the island, of which Donald John's valuable manuscript is one.

'Truth' is a multi-faceted concept and, as with any community, it is impossible for any written account to encompass all aspects of the truth of life on St Kilda. But as we search for the 'truth', it is surely important to pay particular attention to the views of people like Donald John Gillies and his brother, who actually lived on the island as part of the St Kildan community for many years. While it cannot be ruled out that to some extent the Gillieses may have been repeating views about the island which were derived from other writers, or others they had met from outwith the island, it is reasonable to suppose that on central issues such as religion and attitudes towards the evacuation, they are likely to be reflecting the beliefs and assumptions of the community. What they have to say may not support the romantic, fashionable, or critical views of outside observers, but on many topics it is likely to be authentic and therefore worthy of respect by those who are seeking 'the truth'.

Finally, I am grateful for assistance in the editing task from Alison Kennedy, a Gaelic placement student who worked for The Islands Book Trust during Summer 2009. I am also grateful for helpful comments on this introduction while in draft from Bill Lawson, Donald Meek and Michael Robson, none of whom share responsibility for any remaining errors or the views expressed.

JOHN RANDALL
Chairman, The Islands Book Trust

Publisher's Note

As indicated in the editor's introduction, idiosyncratic or inaccurate spellings of some names (even when these are inconsistent with modern usage), and repetition of some parts of text, have been retained in the effort to be faithful to an original piece of testimony.

Brief Chronology for Rev. Donald John Gillies

1901 Born St Kilda, 29 May 1901.

1916 Left school after Grade 6 at age 15.

1924–27 Left St Kilda for Glasgow. After a year working as a deckhand on a dredger in the River Clyde, he began preparing himself to become a missionary by taking courses at the Bible Training College in Glasgow, and a course to improve his English. In 1926 he applied to become a student of the Presbyterian Church of Canada and was accepted early in 1927.

1927–33 In April 1927 he sailed from Glasgow to Quebec City to take up a summer mission charge at North River, Cape Breton, Nova Scotia. In September he began studies at the Presbyterian College in Montreal (McGill University) while fulfilling short-term missionary engagements each summer, first at North River and later in rural charges in Ontario and Quebec.

1933–42 On completion of his divinity degree in 1933 he was ordained in Knox Presbyterian Church, Carberry, Manitoba, where he met his wife, Lillian Gilmore, whom he married on 29 May, 1935. Shortly after this he received a call from the church of North River/North Shore (where he had previously served as missionary) and four years later in September 1939 he was inducted to the neighbouring Cape Breton charge of Mira Ferry/Catalone.

1942–46 Enlisted as an army chaplain with the Pictou Highlanders at Sydney, Nova Scotia, in April 1942 and after service in various parts of Canada was transferred to England early in 1944 to become chaplain for a brief period at the military hospital, Aldershot. He sailed to France later in 1944 to join the 27th Canadian Armoured Regiment as senior protestant padre with the rank of Captain. He served with that regiment in campaigns through Belgium, Holland and Germany where he remained at Wilhelmshaven for six months after hostilities ended in May 1945. After further service in England he returned to Canada in February 1946 and received honorable discharge in Vancouver.

1946–69 His subsequent career as a civilian was spent in British Columbia, first as minister of Vancouver Heights Presbyterian Church from April 1946 until 1952 when he accepted an appointment as Prison Chaplain at the New Westminster Federal Penitentiary. On retirement from this position in 1966 he was inducted as minister of Knox Church, Sooke, British Columbia, where he remained until his retirement from full-time pastoral work in 1969.

1969–93 In his later years he undertook various part-time assignments for the Correctional Division of the Royal Canadian Mounted Police for several years and as Chaplain of the Royal Canadian Legion, Chapter 148 (North Burnaby). He also travelled widely and maintained close contacts with the surviving inhabitants of St Kilda, including visits to Australia and New Zealand where he met various descendants of St Kildan residents. He also took an active part in the St Kilda Club and corresponded regularly with historians and others interested in St Kilda. In August 1980 he returned to St Kilda for the rededication of the recently restored church on the 50th anniversary of the evacuation of the island and preached the sermon in the service to celebrate that occasion.

He died in Vancouver on 5 November 1993 at the age of 92.

The Truth about St Kilda

The Early Years of Our Lives

In our early years we are interested chiefly in the things of the present and those with whom we work and play. Ours is a world of fact and realism, where little or no attention is given to the pages of history but as we grow older and the morning of life reaches high noon, the mind begins to dwell more on the past and to contemplate the future. There comes a desire to know something more than the cross-section of life we call 'Today'. We are no longer satisfied to enjoy years of quiet contentment in the shade of the family tree, without acquainting ourselves with its roots and branches. Delving into the past, we find our early indifference has robbed us of much we would like to know. Parents and grandparents are gone, and with them so much of family history that cannot be recalled.

In my early days I can recall religion and the exercise of the sanctuary were not confined to the House of God and to his Holy day. Their religion was for weekdays as well as for the Sabbath in all the homes on the Island. The family altar was early erected. Here, both morning and evening, gathered the household, each taking part in the singing of the psalms and at times in reading of the Scriptures, then kneeling down to Heaven's Eternal King, the father leading the family in prayer. In reference to the history of the St Kilda congregation, the morning and evening service was conducted wholly in the Gaelic language. Should the missionary discover that some were present who could not understand him in Gaelic, he would give a synopsis of the sermon in English. There was no instrumental music, nor were hymns used. Psalms only were sung in all services, with the exception of the Sabbath School.

The St Kildians owe a great gratitude to one outstanding theologian called the Apostle of the North, Rev. Dr John MacDonald, minister of Ferintosh in the Black Island in the early nineteenth century. He was the first missionary that brought the true message of salvation to the Island according to what I heard discussed on many occasions by my father and grandfather Donald Ferguson at our own fireside. Dr MacDonald made four trips to the Island. His first visit he experienced a very rough crossing from the Sound of Harris to St Kilda which is approximately 55 miles from shore to shore. He could not land on Village Bay so he landed on the north side of the Island which is called Glen Bay. Some Islanders met him and welcomed him to the Island. About seventy feet from where he landed there was a spring of water gushing from a rock. He removed his hat and drank out of this well. The Islanders built a *cleit* over this well and it is still standing and they called the well Eternal, *Tobar Na Mauich*, around 16th September 1822. This was his first visit to St Kilda. On his arrival MacDonald found neither an organised church nor a strong Calvinist religion. There was no house for a missionary, neither a church or a chapel.

'During my stay in the Island', wrote MacDonald, 'the people gathered in a barn'. He preached eleven times and the people responded to his message. I heard it said on more occasions than once that he was shocked at the state of Christianity on the Island. Swearing and taking the Lord's name in vain seemed to be the way the Islanders expressed themselves. A friend of mine who I'm greatly indebted to sent me a copy of a letter by Dr MacDonald to his brother who was a minister at Helmsdale, Scotland.

The First Examination in St Kilda School

The letter goes on to say on one occasion, while staying on the Island for a period, Dr MacDonald visited the day school to examine the pupils. This examination was in the Gaelic language and he describes his experience as follows: 'After examining the more advanced classes among them on the principles of Christianity and particularly the leading doctrines of the gospel, in all of which they gave me much satisfaction, I confined my examinations to the chapter which they had just read and which happened to be the 7th chapter of Luke. I must say that I was astonished to find how smartly and correctly the greater part of them answered the questions put to them, having had no previous notice of my intentions as to the sort of cross examination and therefore no opportunity afforded them of preparing themselves.

My notes on this subject run thus: 'On what message did John the Baptist send his disciples to Christ?' A boy of about fourteen replies: 'To inquire if he was the person who was to come.' 'What do you mean by the person who was to come?' 'The promised Saviour' says he. 'And what reply did Christ give them?' 'He was working miracles at the time and He bade them go and tell John the things that they had seen.' 'How did the miracles which he wrought prove that this was He who was to come?' 'Because', replies another boy, 'none but God could do these things and none except God was with Him'. 'But did not others work miracles as well as Christ?' 'Yes', replied the first boy, 'but not in their own strength. Christ wrought them by His own power'. 'Who is Christ?' 'The son of God', replies a third boy.

He continued to examine the pupils on the love of Christ. This examination was addressed to the senior boys and girls. Thus ended the exercise, and after delivering a short address to the children and parents, he concluded his visit to the school with prayer. One can imagine the expression of satisfaction on Dr MacDonald's face and also on the faces of those parents who obviously were present when the St Kildian children did so well. So this finished the first school examination that took place on the Island well over a hundred years ago.

A Sketch of my Life from Boyhood Days on St Kilda

I was born on the Island of St Kilda on 29th May 1901 at 3 a.m. in a three room cottage consisting of a kitchen and two bedrooms. In the master bedroom there was a fireplace. On exceptionally cold nights fire was lit, which at least took the chill off the room but in the kitchen the fire never went out summer or winter.

There was a long chain coming down the chimney. There was a special hook used for the kettle, pots with handles and also the girdle. The girdle was used everyday of the week to bake scones, with the exception of Sunday. Saturday double dose was baked.

My first recollection of a missionary was at the age of five. I remember him coming to our home at 15 Main Street St Kilda and giving me a candy. His name was John Fraser and strange as it may appear, I met Mr Fraser here in Vancouver 1947. He told me that he had a very happy ministry in St Kilda for three years. He thought a great deal of the Islanders and he paid a great tribute to my father for his devotion to the cause of Christ on the Island. He had a niece of his from Obbe, Harris who stayed on the Island with them in 1906. This niece married a Peter Ross from Embo, Scotland. Peter was a faithful elder here in the Free Church of Scotland Vancouver. Mrs Ross had a heart of gold and she spoke to me time and time again of the happy year she spent on St Kilda. She maintained that the St Kildians were the most hospitable people in the world. A year ago I officiated at her funeral service. She arrived at the age of 91 years. She was laid to rest in the Burnaby Masonic Cemetery, British Columbia.

I started school in the year 1906. As the church was responsible for the education in the school, the missionary and his wife worked as a team in this direction. So my first team teachers were Mr and Mrs Peter MacLachlan who with his charming wife remained on the Island of St Kilda for three years. Peter MacLachlan was an evangelist whose work was closely connected with that of Moody and Sankey. He was a native of the Isle of Mull. Peter would spend the a.m. teaching period. In the afternoon, two to four, his wife would take over. She was a tall woman, kind hearted and well educated. I believe that she was educated at Lincoln and had spent sometime teaching small children at York before marrying Peter MacLachlan at the age of 25.

In 1906 I remember the first school inspector who came to the Island on the passenger steamer SS *Hebrides*, one of MacBrayne's boats. Mr Peter MacLachlan summoned the children to school. I still remember the examination questions that were asked: for standard one, a simple addition, a multiplication and reading the alphabet. I was recommended to standard two. The schoolhouse was attached to the church.

The Method of Heating the School

Each pupil took his turn by carrying one peat to school. The arrangement was made this way: standard one class would be responsible to keep the fire going one day a week then next day standard two.

The school would commence in the a.m. with devotions which consisted of a singing of a psalm and repeating the Lords Prayer. The school would be dismissed with singing of a familiar hymn 'Jesus loves me' or 'Yield not to temptation' or 'God be with you until we meet again'. We were allowed one recess in the forenoon. One game we were taught was hide and seek; we loved this game. We also played football. If my memory served me rightly the attendance in 1906 and 1907 stood at twenty-one. During my term at school, from the age 5 to 15, we had three missionaries as teachers, Mr and Mrs Peter Maclachlan and Mr MacArthur, a native of Tiree. He was a bachelor. A sister kept house for him and occasionally she would take an afternoon teaching. Mr and Mrs MacKinnon, he was a Skye man and his wife was a qualified teacher and she took over in the afternoons. She was certainly a capable teacher and a strict disciplinarian. At the age of ten I was able to repeat the shepherds psalm 23 in Gaelic, the Lords Prayer and the Commandments. My Godly parents who took the vow when I was baptised 'to bring him up in the nurture and admonition of the Lord', and this they did. It was compulsory in the home to memorise that portion of Scripture.

Life and Custom on the Island of St Kilda

Normally during the summer months the inhabitants used to rise around 7 a.m. for breakfast and morning worship. Every home in the village followed this method. The cutting of the peats was to keep the fire burning in summer and winter; this was a must. This chore would take a week cutting and approximately the same time collecting the peats and placing them in the *cleits*.

My father's stock consisted of two cows and a couple of calves. The farm did not yield enough crop to feed that amount of cattle during winter months so we had to gather hay from Islands that had no animals on them. This was a very heavy chore.

At the age of twelve in the year 1913, I can recall an epidemic of flu struck the inhabitants of the Island. In addition to this, the food was practically all gone and I remember our family had to use the potatoes we had set aside for seed. So all the families on the Island experienced this predicament. By a sheer coincidence, who happened to sail into Village Bay but an Aberdeen fishing trawler skippered by a great friend of the Islanders, namely Donald Craig. He immediately sent a distress call to the British Government stating the need of medical aid, and also food supplies. This distress call brought immediate help. The British cruiser HMS *Active* was dispatched with doctors and nurses, and food supplies. The church was turned into a hospital, and the school room was used as a supply room. Food was supplied to all the families on the Island.

Following the HMS *Active*, which arrived around 11th May 1913, on 20th May 1913 the tug *Victor* anchored in the Village Bay unexpectedly with more provision, which was greatly needed, and thankfully received by the natives. Responsible for this was a well known and respected business man by the name of Thomas Lipton, and another great man by the name Sir Joseph Lyons. Lipton is on the lips of all tea drinkers. Lipton's product cannot be matched by any other company that produces tea. From that day on, large quantities of Lipton's tea was consumed on the Island of St Kilda. I remember being present with my uncle Neil Ferguson, William MacDonald, Finlay MacQueen and my father as they approached the missionary in the garden of the manse, Mr MacArthur, to arrange a letter of thanks to be sent to those who arranged for the flour, potatoes, meat, sugar and tea, and many other useful groceries. So a letter of appreciation was dispatched.

That particular winter was a very severe one with snow gales and I'm of the impression the severity of the winter prevented the trawlers from Fleetwood and Aberdeen from visiting us as they used to in the past year. One winter day that year I counted twenty ships of all sizes sheltering in Village Bay; practically all of them were from countries such as Norway, Sweden and France.

[*Birds Found on St Kilda*]

At the beginning of April the first bird to arrive at the Island was the shearwater. During the day on the west side of the Island, on the sea opposite the Carn Mhòr, for a couple of miles the sea would be covered with them.

As a young lad of fifteen years I used to leave home with a couple of the neighbours an hour before dark, arriving at Carn Mhòr as the stars used to appear in the sky. Here we would wait patiently all night. The shearwater would fly ashore approximately an hour before dawn. We had with us a trained dog. These birds used to land with a thump. The dog immediately jumped and was always successful and would come to you with the bird in his mouth. If we caught a half dozen or more we consider it a very successful night, and believe me tasting a fresh bird after feeding on salt mutton, salt fish and salt fulmar, the shearwater tasted delicious.

The next bird to arrive around 1st May was the puffin. If it was a mild April, one could see the sea opposite Soay, Boreray, Glen Bay and Carn Mhòr for miles covered with puffins, millions of them around these places I have mentioned. Studying the habits and shape of this bird as follows: This bird is found in great many places: Bristol Channel on the west coast of England. In 1927, fishing off Bird Island, here I came upon thousands of puffins. Bird Island is 10 miles from Sydney, Cape Breton, Nova Scotia. In 1975 I conducted a tour from Toronto through Ontario, Quebec, New Brunswick, Prince Edward Island and Cape Breton. I came upon a colony of puffins on Bonaventure Island, Quebec.

A. V. C. Wynne Edwards wrote this about the puffin:

> Alone among the auk family, puffins stand up on their legs. It does not occur to most people that the visible joint of a bird's leg bends backwards and is actually the heel, normally raised high off the ground; the real knee is hidden within the contour of the body. The so called leg is thus actually formed from the elongated instep region of the foot, and the foot is nothing but toes; all other auks stand and usually shuffle about, with the heel flat on the ground.

I know for a fact that they are expert divers eating small fish, and by some uncanny faculty they can hold their first fish crosswise in the beak while they catch a second and a third accommodating each one in the same way, until the bill will hold no more when they fly home to feed the youngster. I watched this performance on Boreray and Carn Mhòr and I often wondered how could they manage to hold such a load in their beak. According to the information I gathered they live at sea all winter.

As an Islander, we often discussed this topic as to where the puffin winter. The St Kildians including myself thought that they emigrated to warmer climates and found homes for them similar to the ones they left behind in St Kilda but I discovered a few years ago that those impressions were entirely wrong. They live at sea, often among the ice in the winter. It is interesting to know that after breeding is over, the gaudy sheath of the bill is shed and until it grows again the following spring, the puffin's beak is reduced to no more than half its summer size. Those discarded beaks were prized by the Indians for making necklaces.

In passing I read recently a writer who wrote many articles on the Island quoting the Island women were responsible to go and gather the puffins. During my generation it was entirely the responsibility of the male. At times a man and wife would be together with their dog and the dog would locate the hole where the puffin had his nest. So between the two of them they would kill about 150. Then that 150 would be shared amongst other Islanders that were unable to gather for themselves. The feathers were used for pillows and the surplus was sold to pay part of the year's taxes. However, the puffin barbecued was delicious. As a matter of fact this bird was a very valuable bird as far as the Islanders were concerned; this bird was needed for their survival.

April also was a time to harvest the guillemot. This bird was found on Boreray, Stac Birroch, near the Island of Soay, Stac an Armin and also I noticed the guillemot at Bonaventure Island province of Quebec, Canada. With the method used to catch this bird, you endeavoured to dress as close to the colour of the rock as humanly possible. You selected a ledge and laid on this ledge at night. In the spring of 1918 I recall with the following – Donald MacDonald, Neil Ferguson, John MacDonald, Donald MacQueen and Finlay MacDonald – landing on Boreray for the purpose of harvesting the guillemots.

This was my first experience at this type of capturing the guillemot and I remember being a little bit scared. This bird would fly on to this ledge approximately an hour before dawn. Some would land on you and some close to you. My catch on this expedition numbered 42; others in the party caught more. Some of these young men had done this several times.

Another important bird is called the gannet; these are the largest sea birds nesting in thousands on Stac Lee, close to the Island of Boreray. As our boat approached the stac, the gannets came to meet us in their thousands. (The last time my wife and I experienced this was in July 1976. We were on a Cruise on the P&O Liner *Uganda*.) At one time I heard my father repeating more than once that the gannets were the main food supply of the St Kildian people when he was young. I also heard my father and grandfather discussing the methods in capturing this bird and apparently father took part in this expedition several times. Landing on Stac Lee is not a very easy chore, however; the sea requires to be dead calm. There is a pin stuck to a rock and a rope has to be connected to this pin, then if one is successful in getting the rope around the pin, a man can jump to the ledge. This is the only way landing can be made on Stac Lee. In order to catch this bird, it's at night. There is always a king bird who is the watch king, one has to look for the watch king. If successful in killing the watch king, one can count it a very successful hunt. This bird is not killed with a stick, you catch it by the beak and a little twist of the neck and that's it. He is the easy bird to kill of all the birds on St Kilda.

In reference to the young fulmar, this is a must for winter food. We used to have two casks full of salted fulmars.

1914 War

The First World War brought a remarkable change to living conditions on the Island. The Government placed about thirty men of the Naval Reserve on the Island. They built huts on the southeast side of the church: three sleeping huts, a cook house and a dining hut, and, in addition to these, a hut for the officer in charge.

The wireless transmitting station was completed on 22nd July 1913 and the local missionary Mr MacArthur, a native of Tiree, was taught how to run this wireless. It did not last long in operation when something broke down. There was a Marconi operator in 1913 who remained for a couple of months. I remember the first Sunday in August 1913 this operator entering the church during church service and summoning help to put out a fire that started in the transmitting room. I noticed that his hair was singed with the fire. All the able bodied men left the church immediately and formed a bucket brigade. They were able to confine the fire to one room but extensive damage was done to the walls of the room and to some of the equipment. After the fire, the Marconi operator after a week got the wireless in operation again and left the running of it to the local missionary. However, around 10th November

1913, the wireless broke down and remained dormant. This wireless station became operational the moment the Naval Reserve was placed on the Island in the year 1916, and continued until 18th May 1918 when it was put out of commission by a German submarine who fired 70 rounds, but it became operational again a month after the bombardment.

The headquarters of the Naval Reserve on St Kilda was in Stornoway, Lewis. In addition to this protection of the Naval Reserve stationed on the Island, the Island had also the protection of armed trawlers guarding the Island, but when the crucial moment came on 18th May 1918 there was not a single one of these boats in the vicinity of St Kilda.

The Naval Reserve established a lookout on Oiseval Mountain from daybreak to dusk. In addition to this they continued the same lookout on the Naval base around the clock. In 1916 they recruited four of the natives for a 24 hour lookout on Mullach Mhòr facing Glen Bay, or North Bay as it is sometimes called. The enemy could easily make a landing in this area. Four men signed up for this task, namely Finlay MacDonald, John MacQueen, Neil Gillies and Donald MacQueen, at two shillings a day. St Kilda was a thriving place in this direction. Here for the first time in the history of the Island regular mail was established, mail was leaving the Island twice a week and received twice a week – something that was never heard of before. German submarines were exceptionally busy in the water surrounding the Island. Cargo vessels from various countries were using the route on their way to Canada and America.

Many a vessel in 1915 and 1916 was sunk near the Island. In July 1916 a freighter was sunk approximately northwest of Soay. They landed on a beach near Cambair with twenty of a crew. Here they were spotted by the watch on Mullach Mhòr, Finlay MacDonald. These men were carrying a white flag and they were met by the members of the Naval Reserves who led them to the village. They were natives of Oslo, Norway. They were transported to Stornoway by a Naval vessel that same evening.

18th May 1918 was a beautiful day and the Village Bay was like a pond. Approximately around 7.30 a.m. the Naval man on watch on Oiseval reported that a submarine had surfaced 2 miles from Village Bay but he could not identify the submarine on account of the fact that there was no flag or any mark of identification to identify what country it belonged to. The officer in charge notified the villagers to evacuate their homes, and make for shelter. This they did and I found myself in Ruaval, so I took shelter in a cave. He fired 70 rounds. The first round struck approximately 20 feet from the pier, the second shot struck the church and the third round went about 70 yards beyond his target. His aim and object was to destroy the wireless and this he was able to do on his sixth round. The wireless operator, who was trying his best to get an SOS out, was able to accomplish this, with the result that the wireless operator at Stornoway, which was our Naval headquarters, picked up the distress signal. Whoever that wireless operator was who remained at his post with shells bursting all around him deserved a recognition of some sort for his bravery.

In reference to casualties there were not any but a one-month-old lamb belonging to Neil Ferguson. The civilian storehouse was destroyed with the result that the natives lost fishing lines, nets and buoys. The damage was extensive but I'm in a position to say that the Government reimbursed the Islanders for their loss of fishing equipments. As for Norman MacKinnon, who lived in No. 1 Main Street, the fourth shot struck his home and destroyed the roof and furniture but the Government rebuilt his house and also replaced the furniture.

One lady, who was the missionary's wife, had to remain in the manse, on account of being unable to travel. She had given birth to a baby boy the day before the bombardment took place. Thank God that she and the baby boy survived unharmed, given that 66 shells passed beyond the manse and she was directly in the path of the shelling. I'm sure that the readers of this story would like to know what career this boy took up. I'm delighted to reveal that he graduated as a medical missionary and after graduation he was sent to Africa as a missionary by the United Free Church of Scotland. Unfortunately, this promising young man did not live long. His father, the Rev. Alexander MacKinnon, told me that he was crossing a bridge in Africa and met with an accident and was instantly killed.

The shells from the submarine destroyed many of the Naval huts with the result that they had to use the school house for living accommodation. So I recall that we weren't able to go back to school until 10th December 1918.

Regarding Beach Combing

Whenever a south wind or a southeast, one could rely that timber of all description would land on the beach, especially 2 by 4 inches. I gathered through the winter of 1916 sufficient to put a floor in our kitchen. The original kitchen floor was mud and many other Islanders gathered that amount with the result that they too were able to place a wooden floor in their kitchen. Great many barrels of oil also were located on the beach.

In March 1916 Neil Ferguson, my uncle and the local postmaster, found a 50 gallon cask of rum and every family on the Island received a share of this cask. Regardless of this find, I can truthfully say that I never saw one single man or woman under the influence of drink. I can say with certainty that every home in the Island had on hand a bottle of brandy or whisky, but this was for medical purposes.

[*New Year's Day and Christmas Day*]

New Year's Day was celebrated in this manner: church service at 11 a.m. and after church the Islanders visited homes, especially relatives, and that practically took in every home on the Island. The elderly on this special day took a social drink. Let me say re the 50 gallon cask, one may wonder what happened to it. The Islanders depended entirely on the fishing boats that visited frequently from Aberdeen, Hull and Fleetwood. They brought mail and needed provision, therefore a bottle of spirit in return for this service was very small. The British Government refused to deliver mail or anything to the Island as they maintained that it wasn't their responsibility. A very lame excuse. The Islanders did not celebrate Christmas at all. The children of the Island heard about Santa Claus coming down the chimney with goodies and if we had our stocking set up at the foot of the bed we believed that Santa Claus would fill it. I did, but in the morning rushed over to the stocking and found it empty. Oh what a disappointment it was to me and also to my brother who was two years younger; so we took it for granted that Santa Claus missed our chimney.

[*St Kildians Serving in the First World War*]

Only one to my knowledge, John MacDonald, son of William MacDonald, who lived in No. 3 Main Street St Kilda, was the oldest of the family and he had left the Island and was living in Inverness; so, at the commencement of hostilities, John joined up and was serving in an infantry regiment. On a Monday in August 1916, a Naval drifter came from headquarters in Stornoway with John to see his parents in St Kilda on a 48-hour leave as the regiment he was in was assigned to the Dardanelles in Turkey. On that day all the able-bodied men on the Island were on Soay for the purpose of catching sheep to kill for winter consumption. The factor, who was my grandfather Donald Ferguson, had given the Islanders permission for this kill. Weather being suitable, the Islanders took advantage of this. My father, John Gillies, immediately volunteered that he would go to the Cambair, the nearest point to Soay. The distance separating Cambair and Soay would be approximately a good mile. With a bit of luck and if the wind was favourable, owing to the fact that he had a very powerful voice, he might be able to relate his message to the one that was manning the boat. His trip was successful, with the result that not only did his father return but all the Islanders that were on Soay returned to bid farewell to the only St Kildian serving in the British Army. He saw action in the Dardanelles, but he was one comrade that was fortunate to return without a battle scar. A few years after the war, this young soldier passed on to his eternal reward rejoicing in the Lord. For the few years he lived after the war he was not ashamed to witness for his master. I'm told that his pet theme was 'I'm not ashamed to own my lord or to defend His cause, maintain the glory of His cross, and honour all His laws.'

In the summer of 1917, the waters surrounding the Island were saturated with German submarines. These submarines sunk a number of freighters and their crews landed on the Island in small boats. One day in July 1917, one of the Naval trawlers was attacked and the submarine was able to put this Naval vessel out of action by a direct hit. The trawler made for Village Bay and beached the vessel, a big hole in her bow. I remember the Navy men going from home to home gathering all the cement that they could get and finally they got sufficient to mend this hole and were able to take this boat back safely to headquarters in Stornoway. Here is another instant that the captain of this Naval vessel did not pay the attention he should to his duty. This occurred early in the morning. The gunner of this vessel was in a small boat fishing or hauling in nets with the result that the trawler did not fire a shot. If the captain of this vessel paid attention to his duty there was a strong possibility that he could have destroyed the enemy submarine.

The relationship between the civilian population and the Navy men stationed on the Island was excellent. They took interest in us youngsters, telling us about life on the mainland and the advantages that we would enjoy. They taught us how to communicate with one another at a distance by semaphoring, taught us the alphabet and how to use it by signalling with two flags. Here we were able to relay messages to one another at a distance and also it proved advantageous to relay messages to trawlers in Village Bay when we were unable to reach them on account of the rough sea pounding on our shores, which made it impossible for us to launch our small boats. This happened, I can recall, more than once.

The Navy men also taught every able-bodied man on the Island how to use a rifle and also supplied all the men with rifles and ammunition. We youngsters also learnt from those men how easy it was to make a living on the mainland. They told us that we were working on the Island like slaves and not accomplishing anything. They told us that we could have horses to plough our fields and carts to carry our goods with these horses, goods that we had to carry on our backs and this appealed to us youngsters. These men painted a rosy picture which made us a little discontented with our way of living on the Island, so listening to these stories I vowed when I would arrive at an age to make a living that I would leave the Island, and I did, and I shall relate that story eventually.

After the Bombardment

Approaching Village Bay from the east, the entrance is approximately 2 miles wide and to the south is Stac Levenish. The only inhabitant on that Island is a seabird called the cormorant. I remember as a youngster on the Dun, that is the Island adjacent to St Kilda, coming upon the nest of a cormorant. I discovered that the nest was built of seaweed and sticks and I found three eggs in the nest. I'm told that they feed in the same way as the gannet, thrusting the bill and head down their parents' gullets to pull out the partly digested fish for themselves. I learnt also eggs are laid in May and hatch in the latter half of June. Most of the young have left by the end of August. Levenish is the home of the cormorant and on the east hand side is Oiseval 1,000 ft.

This is the description as you enter Village Bay. As one would expect after the bombardment, four experts arrived on St Kilda and their task was to select the best spot to place a gun. It took them a day to come up with their selected spot, which was southeast of the church on the manse glebe.

The government decided to place a four point seven gun. During the erection of this gun, every able-bodied man was recruited to work on this project at 2 shillings a day, breaking stones and carrying sand. The Islanders never experienced such a change from poverty line to a surplus. The first piece of equipment that was landed was a digging rig. This was the first time any of the Islanders saw such a machine at work. I remember even the females of the Island had to see this digging machine at work. Nevertheless, this machine hastened the building of the ammunition house. It took approximately three months to have the gun installed and ready for action. It was on 11th November 1918 the gun fired its first shot, testing it. I was present at the gun when the testing took place; the first shot struck 40 feet from the pier. I noticed quite a number of dead fish coming to the surface. I have mentioned 11th November 1918 already. Here the First World War came to a close.

The Naval Base was strengthened by adding four gunners. I have a picture of the gun taken on that Memorial Day. It was ready for action and no more use for it. The Naval Reserve was removed from the Island early in 1919. After they left St Kilda, using the term that's often used when a town or a village is deserted by the prosperity it enjoyed for the past four years, now it has become a ghost town. Most of the Islanders now were not prepared to go back to the life and custom they were used to before the 1914 War.

[*St Kildians Leaving the Island*]

The evacuation that took place in the year 1930 commenced in 1920. The population of the Island declined drastically. The largest family on the Island was ten in all, who lived at No. 3 Main Street. They left for Lewis. The two oldest girls married Lewis men who were stationed at Naval Reserve base on St Kilda. Kenneth MacLeod, a native of Lenishader, Lewis, married the oldest girl Anna Bella MacDonald and they lived on the croft at Lenishader. They built a home on the same basis as the St Kildian home. This home was built on a hill and anyone who was familiar with the St Kildians' homes recognised that a St Kildian must live in there. Mary, the second one, married an Alex MacLeod from Point, Lewis. After marriage they emigrated to Melbourne, Australia. Alex passed away but Mary still lives in the area of Melbourne that is called St Kilda. It is interesting to note that thirty families a 100 years ago left St Kilda and settled in that area called after their home Island. In 1900, Rev. MacQueen, one of the emigrants that was among the thirty families that settled in that part of Australia, became a Presbyterian clergy-man, returned to St Kilda and tried his very best to interest some of the natives to emigrate to Australia. Regardless of his persuasion, sorry to say he wasn't able to succeed in influencing a single family.

In addition to this family, the following also left the Island, namely Neil Gillies, John MacQueen, Angus MacDonald and Donald MacDonald. Neil Gillies, Angus MacDonald and Donald MacQueen found employment in Napier shipyard in Old Kilpatrick. John MacQueen found employment with the Clyde Trust Company. Donald MacDonald also worked in the shipyard in Clydebank. He attended the Bible Institution in Bothwell Street, with the result that he qualified to become a missionary in the United Free Church of Scotland. He held pastorates in Islay, Lochportan, Scalpay and Callanish in Lewis. Wherever he served he was well thought of. I remember visiting him in 1937 in Lochportan. His wife was from Obbe, Harris; a very fine and attractive woman who filled the position as a missionary wife in every way, kind hearted and sympathetic. Both of them passed on a few years back.

I'm thoroughly convinced that the main reason for the evacuation in 1930 was lack of manpower. The young folk had left the Island and the elderly that was left was unable to do all the chores that were necessary to keep the fire burning. Islanders depended on the birds for a livelihood. These birds would have to be gathered from the other Islands adjacent to St Kilda, such as the Dun and Soay. Peat cutting and securing it for winter fuel: manpower was not available to do the work as it should be done. This is where the first discontentment arose. The only word I have of praise is to the medical department in Edinburgh, Scotland. Every year they dispatched a doctor, namely Dr Shearer. He examined the school children and he made himself available for anyone who wished to consult him. Also, from time to time they did keep a resident nurse. Nurse Barclay was on the Island in 1930, the year of the evacuation. She was certainly greatly thought of. From 1923 to 1930, thirty-two inhabitants emigrated to the mainland and I left the Island August 1924, so one can derive from this that it was coming to the place. Those who remained on the Island found it very difficult to make a living as they used to, on account of the lack of manpower. The year I left, 1924, the population stood at 66.

[*St Kilda's Parliament*]

Many of the writers have referred to the St Kilda parliament. To my mind none of the writers took part in this parliament that wrote about it, so there was more of a speculation or assumption that what they wrote was its function. I, at the age of seventeen years, started to attend the gathering we call St Kilda parliament so I should be able to give an account of what took place at these gatherings, its function and also the reason for such meeting. Other writers maintain that this parliament met every day except Sunday. I hardly believe that this is 100 per cent true. As certain conditions on the Island did not change that much, as far as certain work that had to be attended to at certain times of the year and this was a must, take for an example peat cutting took approximately ten days – no parliament during that time. The yearly expedition of the Islanders to Boreray to shear the sheep, that's another ten days or so. The parliament did not meet during harvest time, which took at least a fortnight, and I could go on and mention the months that the Islanders fished for ling and also cod, no parliament.

The real purpose of the St Kilda parliament was to see that all the Islanders got their equal share of the cliffs where the fulmar nested. This was just as valuable as the croft you lived on because the fulmar was a part of the Islanders' livelihood.

It was essential for the Islanders to gather and make arrangements who was to be responsible for looking after the bull for a year. One of the Islanders would be appointed at £1 a year as a salary. He visited the sixteen homes during the year and collected a certain amount of hay from each crofter. I can recall him coming to our home and going out to the barn. I had to climb up the loft and throw the hay down. For his method of measurement he carried a string with a notch in it. He measured its width and height.

Another purpose for discussion coming before parliament was if one of the Islanders were to build a barn, a day would be set aside when most of the Islanders were available to help. Another very important item that used to come up for discussion: the needs of the widows and orphans. If a widow needed a *cleit* to be built, a day was set aside for this to be done. In September, this parliament decided as to how many lambs each family could place on the Dun for winter grazing. As a general rule, each family would be allowed eight. Another important matter: an ordained minister visited the Island for the purpose of conducting communion, baptisms and also marriages, so one of the Islanders would be appointed to provide a sheep to the missionary, in order that fresh meat was available for the ordained minister. The Islanders paid him one pound for his sheep. The people had to work together for a great many projects.

So the St Kilda parliament had its merit. One must remember that there was not a single store on the Island. Therefore this parliament had to see that there was flour, especially oatmeal, stored in the factor's storehouse and also sufficient lumber that was suitable to make coffins. The inhabitants were a very community-minded people, worked together; the new saying that has become on the scene in the last few years. Those who prayed together will remain together and I can say without any hesitation the word that fits the people of St Kilda, young and old, is togetherness.

[*Fishing Industry on St Kilda*]

Re the fishing industry on St Kilda, there were four boats operated by oars and sail. The fishing season commenced from the middle of July to the end of August. These small boats had a crew of five, which accommodated all the men that were able to fish. The fishermen as a general rule used eels for bait. We used to start baiting the lines round about one in the afternoon, weather permitting, and we used to sail out of Village Bay round about 4 p.m. We used to go as far as 3 miles from the Island, west of the Island of Dun. The lines were set at dusk and very often we would sail to the nearest cave at the back of the Island of Dun and at daybreak we used to be at the lines. As a matter of fact, fishing as a general rule was good, arriving back home round 9 a.m., fished, cleaned, salted and, weather permitting, returned to fishing ground next night. This was the procedure and we continued this routine while the weather lasted.

[*Mr A. G. Ferguson*]

My uncle, Alex G. Ferguson, had a boat on the Island and this boat was named *The Ferguson Boat.* He left the Island of his birth in 1892. Immediately upon arriving in Glasgow, he attended night school, after working a couple of years in a grocery store. From his work in this grocery, he got the idea that he could set up his own business and be independent. This he did and was very successful as a tweed merchant. He set up office at 93 Hope Street, Glasgow. He dealt not only in St Kilda Tweed but also in Harris Tweed. He travelled Uist, Harris and Lewis with the result that he was selling tweed called Harris Tweed.

He was one that helped a great many Islanders arriving in Glasgow as strangers. Here he would take them to his home and kept them free of charge until he found work for them. When I arrived in Glasgow in 1924, I remained in his home for two weeks in Old Kilpatrick until he found employment for me in the Clyde Trust Company. This man did for the St Kildians more than any other living being. Visitors from St Kilda who had to attend hospital or visit a medical doctor; he saw to it that they were looked after until they returned back to the Island.

He was very fond of his native Island and returned to it every summer for three weeks or so. The moment he would arrive on the Island, he would gather five young lads age 17 and 18 and taught them to be fishermen. He would be out at sea everyday that he was on the Island, weather permitting, fishing ling. After the fish was sold, he would share the proceeds among the fisher lads that he had that summer. I heard my mother discussing also the first letter he wrote and it was regarding the disaster that struck the Island in the year 1886. A terrible storm swept over the Island causing considerable damage to crops and property. My mother was the oldest of the family, Annie Ferguson. He was the second oldest of the family. My mother could not speak a word of English apparently. Some kind of a school was established on the Island and met in the factor's house. School was not compulsory at that time and I'm of the impression that the elderly Islanders did not consider school to be of great importance. Building a *cleit* or gathering puffin's eggs was more important. Under such circumstances my uncle's first letter to my mind was a masterpiece, regardless of grammatical mistakes in spelling.

Here is a copy of the letter that was written and sent by my uncle, A. G. Ferguson, 24th September 1883. A 'mail boat' was washed up on the beach near Aird, Uig, in Lewis, apparently the message was written on a sheet of paper torn from a school exercise book. This letter was addressed to Kenneth Campbell, a trader at Lewis: 'My Dear Sir, I'm now going to write you a letter, and sending her in one of the little ships in which we were sailing on the shore as you know, to let you know all the news. The men were building a house, just a little house, for the cows. A great storm came on and all the corn and barley were swept away by the storm and one of the boats was swept away by the sea. The men of St Kilda is nearly dead with the hunger. They send two boats from St Kilda to go to Harris, not the fishing boats, but little piece of wood like the little one which I send. I send my best love unto to you. I am yours truly, Alexander Ferguson.'

The minister on the Island, Rev. John MacKay [also sent a letter], but he addressed his letter to Dr Rainy, a Principal of the Theological College of the Free Church in Edinburgh and also pastor of Hope Street Free Church, Glasgow. I attended this church in 1926. Dr Rainy passed on to his eternal reward and a Rev. John MacLeod OBE was his successor. Dr Rainy's letter also arrived in Lewis a week before my uncle's letter. Dr Rainy immediately got in touch with the British Government for food supplies to be sent to St Kilda. Eventually relief was sent to the Island St Kilda: corn, barley, meal and potatoes delivered by the SS *Hebridean.* This ship was a cargo and a passenger boat sailing from Glasgow with tourists and cargo calling at such ports as Oban, Tobermory, Coll, Tiree, Castlebay, Lochmaddy and St Kilda; ten day trip for £10, which included everything. Another passenger boat carried tourists and cargo as far as St Kilda, the SS *Dunara Castle*, Fare £10 for a ten day trip.

My uncle A. G. Ferguson, a self-educated man who travelled extensively on account of his tweed market, he was a true St Kildian citizen. He established a home in Old Kilpatrick, Glasgow, which he was greatly proud of, one of kindness, loyalty and friendship. Where father and mother had great respect for one another, love prevailed and children wanted; where the simplest food is good enough for kings because it is earned; where money is not so important as loving kindness; when even the tea kettle sings for happiness. That is the type of home my uncle and aunt established in Old Kilpatrick, Glasgow; a home that was a haven to many an Islander, not only from St Kilda but from all parts of the Highlands. It was at his own fireside that one got to know my uncle A. G., as he was known at his best, as nothing pleased him better than to be host to friends and strangers, and share with them the hospitality of a good Highland tradition. He was well liked by all who came in contact with him. His knowledge of Highland Scottish tradition was unlimited. His family consisted of a girl, Susan, Donnie, Alaster and Neil. Donnie, who was a medical doctor, passed away early in life and also Alaster, who was a draughtsman. Susan and Neil are still living in Scotland. My uncle passed away quite a number of years back. My aunt still lives in Dumbarton. A great man in every sense of the word, a great businessman, fisherman and sailor.

[*The Month of September*]

The month of September proved to be a very important month in the life of the population of Hirta. Each family tallied up as to the amount of fish, mutton, fulmar and gannets were required to be salted in barrels for winter consumption. During September, we fish and went to Boreray and Soay for sheep that were fat and ready to kill. This was a very important chore to see that you had sufficient to carry on through the winter month until the spring.

[*Fishing Trawlers*]

Scotland had a law that fishing trawlers fish beyond the three mile limit. As far as the St Kildians were concerned their hands were tied as far as three miles limit was concerned. Fishing trawlers from Hull, Fleetwood, Aberdeen and Grimsby fished within the three mile zone. These fishing vessels were the ones that brought mail and provisions to the Island from September to June of the coming year. An Islander would not dare to report those vessels who were violating laws. Those trawlers were the only link that the Islanders had with the mainland. As far as the Government of Great Britain was concerned they weren't interested in the Island unless an emergency arose. The Islanders many times petitioned the Government to establish a steady mail service to the Island summer and winter. I can recall one answer that the Government sent to the Island. 'His Majesty's Government regrets to be unable to comply with your request as the Island is in private hands. Therefore we feel that it's their responsibility to furnish the Island with daily mail.'

The Islanders felt greatly provoked at the Government to arrest one of these trawlers whom they found fishing within the three mile limit. The cruiser *Mina* did this arrest so the trawler was taken to Stornoway. Two St Kildians accompanied the captain of the trawler and in court in Stornoway they pleaded with the judge to set this captain free on account of his kindness to the Islanders supplying provisions, bringing mail to the Island and taking mail from the Island. On account of this, the judge did take the plea of the St Kildians into account when passing judgement so the fine was greatly reduced. So the two St Kildians were proud of themselves because of this achievement.

[*Holy Communion*]

The great event of the year, as far as I can ascertain, was the celebration of Holy Communion. This took place on the Island once a year during the summer month. The Islanders looked forward to this celebration more than anything else. Prayer meetings took place in the church months before the arrival of the ordained minister that the United Free Church of Scotland appointed to dispense communion on the Island. Marriages also took place and baptisms after the celebration of Holy Communion. From Thursday till Monday evening these services continued almost without intermission, the nights being given to prayer, praise and exhortation.

Thursday was called the day of fasting, in Gaelic *La Traisg*. This day was treated on the Island as a Sunday. We had to see that there was sufficient water in the house to last the day and shoes had to be polished the night before. As a matter of fact the day was observed by the faithful who abstained entirely from food until the afternoon, and then indulged only in slight refreshment. Friday was known as the question day, *La Ceist*; 'after the preliminary singing, and the invocation of the divine blessing, the minister called for the question'. Immediately some elderly noted Christian inquirer stood up, read or quoted a Bible verse, and asked for its interpretation which virtually meant a differential diagnosis between saints and sinners. The minister invariably led off in the discussion that followed and then from a list previously prepared called upon those who addressed the congregation. Let it be understood that no definite information of the special topic under consideration could possibly be acquired previous to its announcement by the one who presented the text.

I remember the last one that I attended and those who took part in the discussion of the topic before them. These men spoke as to their familiarity with the Bible and with Christian experience: Finlay MacQueen, Norman MacKinnon, Malcolm MacDonald, William MacDonald, Neil Ferguson, Angus Gillies, Finlay Gillies,

Donald MacQueen, Ewen Gillies, Donald MacDonald, Donald Gillies, John Gillies and the last name to be called was my grandfather Donald Ferguson, an elder of long standing, a capable and a talented speaker. So on *ceist* day he was always counted as one of the most effective and interesting speakers; all felt that the *ceist* was only touched superficially until Donald Ferguson had his say.

This service lasted from 11 a.m. to 2 in the afternoon; the evening service 6 p.m. It usually lasted an hour and a half. On Saturday afternoon, at the conclusion of the preaching for the day, the candidates for sacramental admission presented themselves for examination as to their knowledge of the doctrines of the gospel, their experience of its saving power, and their performance of religious duties. Many and trying were the questions put and answered. All the elders present in the session room examined the candidate. I heard that in some Highland congregations candidates that presented themselves to become members of the church were put back for another year. As far as I know this never happened on the Island of Hirta, as it is often called. Matters reached their culmination on Sunday when the sacrament was dispensed. The four seats near the pulpit covered with a white cloth constituted four tables. The precentor, William MacDonald, rose and sang one verse of the 103rd psalm to the tune Dundee. Men and women, mostly past middle age, rose up from their seats and, while the first verse of the 103rd psalm was being sung,

O m' anam beannaich thusa nis
An Dia Iehòbhah mòr,
Moladh gach nì an taobh staigh dhìom
Ainm naomha mar as còir

English:
Bless the Lord, O my soul,
And all that is within me,
Bless his holy name!

proceeded to the white covered communion table. As I look back at that Communion Sunday on the Island Kirk, I say nobody could gaze upon these people without being impressed with their sincerity and seriousness, with their conviction that their experience was a blessed reality and not a vanishing dream. It was one of the most grand and sublime sights in the world ever beheld, and compelled one to think of Him who preached to the multitude on the shores of Gennesaret with the ripple of the waves on the strand as the undertone of the words of Life fell from his lips. This was the big yearly event in the life of the Islanders. I have read of writers who placed the great event as the Tourist Ships arriving in Village Bay. Although that was of great importance, it would not surpass the Sacrament of the Lord's Supper that the whole population of St Kilda looked forward to, as they called their spiritual banquet. At the commencement of the Sacrament season the elders met in the church for service at 8 a.m. on Thursday, 8 a.m. on Friday, 8 a.m. on the Sunday. Communion closed on Monday in a thanksgiving service that commenced at 6 p.m. and finished round about 7.45 p.m. The ordained Minister was in charge of services at 11 a.m. Thursday, 6 p.m. Friday, 11 a.m. and 6 p.m. Saturday, 11 a.m. After the Service those who contemplated to become members [were examined]. Sabbath communion at 11 a.m. and 6 p.m. and Monday night, 6 p.m.

[*Weddings and Wedding Customs*]

There was another very impressive Service that I witnessed in the Kirk, three couples getting married at the same time. The whole Service was conducted in the language of the Island, Gaelic. My oldest brother, Donald, was married to Christene MacKinnon that lived with her mother at No. 13 Main Street, St Kilda. Neil Gillies, No. 7 Main Street was united in marriage to Katherine MacDonald who lived at No. 16 Main Street and the third party was John MacDonald, who lived at No. 9 Main Street, was united in marriage to Christene MacQueen who resided at No. 2 Main Street and was a daughter of the great cragsman, Finlay MacQueen. This wedding took place August 1916. Each couple had a best man and a matron of honour. Neil Gillies had his brother-in-law, Angus, and matron of honour was the groom's sister. Donald Gillies had a cousin for a best man and the bride had as a matron of honour a school chum, and a great friend of hers, a Mary MacDonald, who lived at No. 8 Main Street. John MacDonald had as his best man his brother-in-law, and as a matron of honour, a sister of the bride. The bride dress was an ordinary one, home spun, missing the white dress that is customary today. No friends present whatsoever. The corsage was unknown. The wedding service commenced with a psalm singing led by the precentor, a reading and a sermon which lasted for half an hour. The Service lasted an hour and fifteen minutes. This was the end of the wedding, the celebration having taken place already. This celebration takes place a week before the wedding. This was called the *rèiteach.* An invitation was extended to one and all on the Island by the Bride's Father. Tables were gathered from the neighbours; four tables would cover the whole of the kitchen. On this occasion I can recall four sittings in order to accommodate the invited guests who were served mutton, bannock, cheese and tea. This was the custom on the Island of St Kilda in 1916. Even members of the Naval Reserve were invited on this occasion. As soon as they were married the couple went home. That was the end of the wedding. No strong drink or soup served. Judging from the weddings of today, one would be inclined to think that the St Kildians were doing things in reverse. Nevertheless that was the custom of that day and they adhered to it religiously.

In reference to the wedding that took place on the Island in the summer of 1890 that caused quite a stir not only on St Kilda but also in England and Scotland. As a matter of fact this wedding made Headlines in the Scottish, and English papers. I read the version of various writers and their opinion in reference to what took place. Some of the writers were blaming the St Kildians for their ignorance in this matter. A party in England heard that a wedding was to take place on St Kilda. The wedding was that of Annie Ferguson who was attractive, and for this reason she was called a Queen. This was the first time in the history of St Kilda that anyone was called a Queen. This Queen was to be united in marriage to a John Gillies. This couple happened to be my parents. I have heard this story from my Grandfather, Donald Ferguson, and also from my parents. A warm-hearted man with the best intentions, called Ian Campbell, chartered a steamship for the occasion and he also went as far as advertising this expedition in the British papers. He received gifts of all description to take with him to the Island of St Kilda to attend this wedding. Even a white dress was secured for the bride for this special occasion. A dress of that colour the St Kildians had never heard of, neither did they ever hear of a wedding cake. So all these things were entirely new to the Islanders. This was done and the Islanders knew nothing about it. So, as I mentioned before, one would be inclined to think that the inhabitants were doing things in reverse, with the celebration first, and the wedding last. This arrangement of Ian Campbell was made without consulting the party that was to be married. A change was impossible as far as the Islanders were concerned. They were accustomed to their own way of life and they were not going to change overnight.

My Father, who was to be the groom, was a very religious man from his youth up, professing his faith in the Lord, and until the very end of his sojourn on earth he was in walk and conversation a beautiful example of the power of Divine Grace. Nobody could be long in his company before being made aware that here was a man who lived close to his God – a man, who had dedicated his life to his Saviour. He was a man of prayer. Every evening he would spend fifteen minutes in prayer. After tea he would rise from the tea table and retire to the Barn every night. He died in the year 1925, leaving one conviction in the minds of those close to him that for him to die was gain.

Now my Mother's Father was an Elder in the Kirk and a good one at that. As a speaker he was clear and solemn. His words were carefully weighed and he spoke from the depth of his own large experience. In appearance he was tall and well proportioned. His features were dark and wore a calm and mild expression. To a stranger he might appear somewhat reserved, but under the slight austerity was a heart of warm affection and of a genial kindly nature. When he saw some of the gifts for the young couple, and especially seeing a large American organ – an organ he considered to be an instrument of the Devil – there and then he made the decision that no wedding would take place until the boat left Village Bay. He did not want to have any part with those who made the arrangements to change the Island's method to have a celebration after the wedding. Apparently when this boat arrived in Village Bay the natives thought that it was an ordinary boat-load of tourists, but when the natives discovered the purpose of their visit and set eyes upon their great pile of useless offerings, they reacted strongly and refused to let the people of Sunderland [which was where the passengers came from] stay for the wedding. The presents were all rejected and only when the boat had gone was the couple married without fuss on account of their religious beliefs. There was no other alternative but the course of action they took.

I'm thoroughly convinced that if the bride's father would have been informed of all this, he would have simply put a stop to it before the boat left Sunderland. Those that organised this boat trip left the impression with the natives that it was more or less for a show and this was certainly against their religious conviction and they would not have anything to do with it. However, before the evacuation things changed on the Island, and for the first time in the history of St Kilda a wedding took place in the St Kilda Kirk and the Bride wore a wedding white dress. This was my first cousin, Neil Ferguson, son of the postmaster of St Kilda and the first Bride to wear a white dress was the daughter of Finlay MacQueen who lived at No. 2 Main Street. Mary was her name and the oldest daughter, a very industrious person. To my knowledge, I can only recall one 50th wedding anniversary [of a St Kildian] and that was my brother Donald's who was married in August 1916 in the Kirk on the Island. A celebration to mark this occasion took place [1966] at the home of his youngest daughter,

Rachel, Mrs. Johnston, who resides at 157 Shakespeare Ave, Clyde Bank, Glasgow, Scotland. She and her older sister prepared this affair. I happened to be in Glasgow at the time. Quite a number of the St Kildians gathered for this special occasion from Culross, Ben Nevis, Bowling and Kincardine. I believe that this couple were the only ones to arrive at fifty years [of marriage] in the history of St Kilda.

In reference to the other two couples that were married at the same time in 1916, John MacDonald, No. 9 Main Street that married Christene MacQueen, only lived two weeks. John met with a tragic accident the first day of the Fulmar season at the back of Connacher. He and Ewen Gillies that lived in No. 12 Main Street were in partnership killing the young Fulmars. Ewen descended down the cliffs while John was holding the rope as the anchor man. Apparently Ewen slipped and John wasn't secured as he should have been, with the result that he was dragged over the precipice into the Sea and his body was never found, but the body of Ewen was found on a rock and lowered into a boat. He is buried in the St Kilda cemetery.

The other couple was Neil Gillies and Catriona Macdonald. Neil died in an Oban Hospital before the evacuation took place. His widow, Catriona, lives in Lochaline with her son. She is the oldest St Kildian living, well over 90, a remarkable lady. So that's the story of the last weddings that I witnessed in my native Island.

Burial Services of the Island

In the Factor's storehouse east of the manse a certain amount of lumber suitable to make caskets was kept in this storehouse, and the moment death took place, three men, and sometimes four, were given the task of making the coffin, and during my day, from what I saw, the coffin made was painted black. This chore would take almost a day. When completed the coffin was carried to the house of mourning. All the population of the Island would gather to the house. The missionary would conduct worship and at the conclusion of the worship, the remains were placed in the coffin which was then nailed – I witnessed this. No work on the Island took place until the burial. As a general rule all this would take approximately three days. School and work would return to their normal routine on the fourth day. At the grave-side the missionary conducted worship; if the missionary was not available, the Kirk Elder would take his place. In 1913 it was customary to have a wake. This meant that a sheep would be killed and those who attended the wake shared in the eats. I remember that a prayer meeting took place practically all night. In 1916 the custom of 1913 vanished; no sheep was killed, the wake disappeared, close relatives remained with the family until the body was carried to its last resting place.

Quite a number of my relatives are buried in the Island Cemetery – Father's youngest brother who died at the age of 30; there is another brother who died at the age of 10. I have no recollection of this, but my parents showed me the grave. My Grandmother on my Father's side and also on my Mother's side, are buried there. I was told by Angus Gillies that 150 years ago burial on the Island was vastly different to my age, according to the account of a clergyman by the name of Rev. MacKenzie. When an islander died, and if he was reasonably well off, a big celebration of feasting would take place for a week; couple of sheep would be slaughtered – the women of the Island were kept busy baking scones. Apparently the custom in those days was that the moment the coffin was lowered into the grave and the grave filled, the men then would sit down in the cemetery and have a very hearty meal of mutton. And according to the information I received from my friend Angus, they used to send a portion of the mutton over to the home of the deceased, so that the women who baked and worked hard would have a share of it. Thank God that this custom disappeared before my day.

[*The Island Church*]

The Apostle of the North, Dr. MacDonald, was responsible for having the Church built, School house and Manse. The capacity of the Church was for a hundred. There were sixteen seats [pews], eight on the east side and eight on the west side, two seats on the east side of the pulpit, one for the missionary family and the other seat was set aside for strangers.

There was a huge pulpit and below there was a small pulpit for the precentor. As you enter the Church the seats on the west side belonged to the following, the MacCrimmon and Grandfather Donald Ferguson and his sister Margaret, Seat No. 1. Seat No. 2 was John Gillies seat, my Father. No. 3 seat, Donald Gillies who lived in No. 14 Main Street. No. 4 seat belonged to widow Christine MacKinnon, No. 5 Ewen Gillies, No. 6 Finlay Gillies, No. 7 William MacDonald Family, the precentor, No. 8 John MacDonald, No. 9 Main Street. Family pews on the east side as you enter the Church. No. 1 Neil Ferguson, postmaster, No. 2, Lachlin MacDonald, No. 3, Malcolm MacDonald, No. 8 Main Street. No. 4, Christine MacQueen, widow, No. 5, Finlay MacQueen, No. 6, Norman MacKinnon, No. 7, Angus Gillies, No. 8, Donald MacQueen. The Services on Sabbath took place at 11 a.m. and 6 p.m., prayer meeting Wednesday, and this meeting was attended just as good as Sunday morning; every one attended, with the exception of one woman who was mentally ill. Then a monthly thanksgiving service at 11 a.m.; no school that day. Also a quarterly service was held at 11 a.m. The only time that the prayer meeting was cancelled was during sheep shearing which would take approximately a week. By my first recollection ladles were used to take up the collection. But it was changed before I left the Island. There was a stand as you entered the Church so that you dropped your collection into this box, usually halfpenny or a penny.

In the July issue of the *Scots Magazine* 1979 [there is an article] under the heading 'Allen Aitken's Last Voyage to Hirta', the main island in the St Kilda group. Allan is a close friend of mine. I'm greatly indebted to him, and not me alone, but all the living natives of the Island of St Kilda for his interest in restoring at least some of the dwelling homes on Hirta. His restoration of the Church is a magnificent accomplishment, the most important building on the Island, The Lord's House. Reading the following account of the restoration of the Church: 'Now in 1979 – one year before the

50th anniversary of the evacuation of the native population, one working party in particular has an important task. They plan to finish renovation work on the Church – a task dear to Allan Aitken's heart – and after that Allan is contemplating on retiring from the working party programme he launched twenty-one years ago. The Church and the adjacent School without a shadow of doubt played a leading part in the lives of the inhabitants of the St Kildians. As far as the Islanders were concerned the Church was the most important building on the Island. They consider it in this manner, and rightly so. This is none other than the House of God and the very gate of Heaven. Formal Education as it would be recognised today began in 1884 and the School house was completed in 1884. Nevertheless School commenced earlier than 1884. My reference is to a letter my uncle wrote in 1883 [? – *the 3 is unclear in the original* – ed] – and arrived on a beach in Aird Uig in Lewis addressed to an Ian Campbell. It indicates that English was taught on the Island although it wasn't compulsory, but my three uncles took advantage of it, Alex, Donald and Neil Ferguson. My Mother, Annie, who was the oldest of the family missed this opportunity as she was unable to write, read or speak English.

The Church, measuring 30 ft long and 18 ft wide, was built in the year 1830, after the Rev. John MacDonald of the Free Church, who was widely known as the Apostle of the North, visited St Kilda and became deeply concerned about the spiritual welfare of the people. It is worthy of noting according to satistics [*word unclear* – ed] under the direction of the Rev. Neil MacKenzie, who was appointed to St Kilda in 1829. The Society for Propagating [Promoting] Christian Knowledge and the then proprietor the MacLeods of Dunvegan built the [present] church and manse in 1899. The church was renovated and the floor levelled. I remember seeing two stone masons repairing the wall around the manse. The MacLeods of Dunvegan arranged for these repairs to be made and a couple of repair men visited the Island every summer with the result that the walls around the church property were kept in an excellent shape.

William MacDonald was responsible for calling the people to worship by ringing the bell, seeing that eight lamps were lit and the chimneys clean. Few years ago I had the privilege of visiting his oldest daughter in Lenishader, Lewis. She spoke of her father as a religious man. After the congregation left the church he saw the lights out. But what impressed Annie the most was that her father never left the church without kneeling in prayer. Adding my own say re our precentor, he was pre-eminently a man of prayer. As a young man I was greatly taken to him. At times when he was blessed with freedom of expression, it was noteworthy how aptly he employed the language of Scripture. Every quotation was perfectly rendered and faultlessly appropriate. Listening to him on such occasions reminded one of Jacob at Peniel, clinging with intense earnestness to the angels for the blessing. He was a gifted man in prayer. In the July of 1979 in the *Scots Magazine* was a picture of Allan Aitken on his knees varnishing the pulpit. One year before the fiftieth anniversary of the evacuation of the native population, one working party in particular has a poignant task. They plan to finish renovation work on the church; a task dear to Allan Aitken's heart. After this task is completed he contemplates to retire from the working party programme he launched twenty-one years ago.

[*Mrs MacKinnon, School Mistress*]

There were many able school mistresses but to my mind one who attained the highest standard was a Mrs MacKinnon, the wife of the missionary but before her marriage to the missionary she was a qualified teacher. Mrs MacKinnon was a born teacher and all the pupils loved her and all of us were always anxious to please her. In her teaching she inspired a healthy spirit of competition for striving to be at the top of the class. She was exceptionally kind and if any child was feeling under the weather they were taken to sit by the lovely peat fire to get warm. No doubt at times there were many excuses to get that privilege.

One outstanding thing she impressed on me and today I admire her for it; she was a stickler for good manners, and taught us good behaviour. I was so well grounded before I left to go into standard five. The schoolhouse was only one large room and you can imagine the month of November, cold and most of us on our bare feet, nothing to heat it but a big peat fire at the far end. I shiver yet when I think of it, us senior pupils in the back seats near the door that enters into the church and directly in front of us the door of the schoolhouse leading in from the street. Those of us sitting in the back seats near these doors were nearly frozen on cold winter days. I remember the thrill it was when we were called up to the table when the school mistress stood in front of the fire to have our reading session.

She had six different classes. While one class did the reading, the others were set to composition, arithmetic or simply copy writing. She had a very methodical way of teaching. She also was fond of music, which she taught at odd times. The morning session was always devoted to assembling to the singing of a psalm and reading of a chapter of the Bible. Some days I can recall she would have each pupil reading a verse at a time. In being honest and looking back to those days, I was always glad when that was over. If the reading was about Moses, David, Daniel or Saul – anything with the spice of adventure I always liked another story. One other habit I can recall and a routine that was continually followed: I had to repeat from memory a verse from one of the psalms and a question from the shorter catechism.

[*Friday afternoons*]

Every Friday afternoon the school was closed with the singing by the pupils of the last verse of the last paraphrase to the tune Kilmarnock:

> Oh may we stand before the Lamb,
> when earth and seas are fled
> and hear the Judge pronounce our name
> with blessings on our head.

Some Fridays we sang psalm 100 to the tune of Old Hundreth:

All people that on earth do dwell,
Sing to the Lord with cheerful voice,
Him serve with mirth his praise forth tell,
Come ye before Him and rejoice.

We finished the week with the following words: 'The Lord watch between me and thee while we are absent one from another.'

It is easy to look back with nostalgia on those days, days gone by, and compare them with the rush and anxiety of today's desire for speed and more speed in the manner of living but time marches on and the pace gets quicker each year.

July 1979, I had two nieces who visited the Island of their birth, Catherine and Rachel, who attended the one large school room. Another teacher and missionary was a Mr John MacLeod, a native of Uist. His first introduction to the Island was when he was serving as a chief steward on the SS *Hebrides* in 1926. In 1927, the United Free Church of Scotland appointed him as missionary to Hirta. He was an able preacher; of him it could truthfully be said, there was no chasm in his life between precept and practice. Sound judgement and great common sense, combined with true piety characterised him through life. The Islanders were very fortunate to have Mr Dugald Munro [his successor as missionary] as their spiritual adviser when they were negotiating with the British Government to remove them from their native Island. Mr Dugald Munro played a big role to achieve this end. The Islanders were very grateful to him for his great contribution and sound advice. He was a teacher that was well liked by all the pupils. During my sojourn in Scotland during World War Two, I happened to meet one of the ministers that was present at his funeral who very appropriately quoted the words of David in reference to Abner: 'Know ye not that there is a prince, and a great man fallen this day in Israel.' I heard mother saying that Dugald Munro was indeed a great man.

[*Life after Completing School*]

I left school at the age of fifteen in 1916 after completing standard six and, as far as the St Kilda school was concerned, you could not go any further; there was no way of furthering your education. Money was scarce, and you could not afford to emigrate to the mainland to continue your education. One would require to have cash to pay for room and board and no Islander had this kind of money. One worked for a whole year at fishing and gathering fulmars for their feathers and oil. The wool that the farm produced would be in the neighbourhood of eight pieces at the most, 28 yards long and 28 inches wide; worked at this all winter, carding, spinning and weaving. This was shipped to the mainland during the summer month. Received in exchange for this: twelve bags of floor, bag of sugar, tea, shoes, shirts, underwear, soda, dishes, knives and forks. All these things had to be secured by the last mail boat that visited the Island in the latter part of August. There were no stores on the Island.

Gladstone pension cheque to the elderly, aged 70 and over, was five shillings a week. In order to have a little bit of cash one needed to sell to the tourists such articles as socks, sheep, skins, bird eggs for souvenirs, gloves and odd piece of St Kildian Tweed. This was the only ready cash that the natives had. You needed this for church collection, stamps, and if you discovered that an essential article was missing, if by chance that a trawler from Fleetwood, Hull or Aberdeen came to Village Bay on its way homeward bound and was planning a return visit, you ordered those things that you were in great need of. Believe me it wasn't an easy life. It seems to me that it was from hand to mouth. Nevertheless, while there I was very content, and reasonably happy.

[*Sundays and Religion in the Home*]

Sunday was a very quiet, long day for me. In the morning and evening, cows were milked, I was not allowed to pick flowers, or go for a long walk on Sunday. I remember sitting on the grass a very short distance from home occasionally on a very warm Sunday and I used to sleep for a while. My parents would not allow me to sing hymns, only psalms. In the evening after returning from church, chores were done.

Mama taught me the Shorter Catechism in Gaelic. I also had to memorise various chapters of the Bible, reciting glibly without the least understanding of the sentences. When I questioned mother about the Bible, she curtly told me to learn my Bible lessons and be good always. That was the main concern of life. I know that my mother was very naïve; she did not read anything but the Gaelic that was in the United Free Church Record. She would not read any but religious books: the book of Rev. Robert MacCheyne's sermons was well worn.

Mother and father would not allow a pack of cards in the house; mother declared that Satan was in every pack. I remember that my younger brother and I found a pack of cards in a discarded box at the back of the factor's house. After school my brother and I and two cousins met in widow MacKinnon's home, No. 13 Main Street, and played with these cards. Widow MacKinnon did not mind at all. One afternoon who would arrive at this home but the missionary Alexander MacKinnon and here we were in the midst of a game of whist. He just made a bee line for the cards, caught the pack and threw it into the fire. So quietly we left the house greatly disappointed, and I do not recall that we ever touched a pack of cards while we remained on the Island.

I was always interested in history. Robert the Bruce was my hero, as I loved to recite the Battle of Bannockburn. In school I was greatly complimented on this accomplishment by the teacher Mrs A. MacKinnon, the missionary's wife, a school teacher that I thought the world of. I remember one day my mother taking me to task, noting that I did not read the Bible so much lately, 'Why don't you read the Scriptures as you used to do?' I read the Bible and being honest because there was nothing else to read. I remember saying to her in Gaelic, 'I cannot make head or tail of some books in the Old Testament; Chronicles and Kings repeat and contradict.'

The answer on that occasion made a great impression on me: 'It may seem so to you for you do not understand. It's an old saying when you eat fish don't eat the bones or you may be choked.' She went on placidly, 'There is so much good in the Bible, you need not question what you don't know.'

Yes, I agree, there is the Book of Esther. It is a beautiful story of a woman's love for her people yet God is not mentioned once in the entire Book, not even once. Granpa Ferguson says it was almost excluded from the Bible for that reason, yet Esther risked her life for her God and her people, so it was included. The next question I asked mother, 'Do you believe Jonah was swallowed by a whale?' 'Of course I believe Jonah was in a whale for three days', she replied, 'The Bible says that God prepared a great fish for that purpose. I'd believe Jonah swallowed a whale if the Bible said so.' To finish her argument, she said you just look to the last page of the Bible, 'Thou shall not add or take from this book.' This is the way she said it, *'Agus ma bheir neach air bith o bhriathran leabhar na fàidheadaireachd seo, bheir Dia a chuibhreann-san à leabhar na beatha. Ma chuireas neach air bith ris na nithean seo, cuiridh Dia airsan na plàighean a tha sgrìobhta annsan leabhar seo.'*

Mother and father were certainly well versed in Scripture. Father could repeat from memory the 53rd chapter of Isaiah and chapter 55 and 60, and New Testament Gospel according to St John chapter 14. He repeated all these without a stop. No wonder, they were often at the greatest Book in the world and a great many of the males of St Kilda were well versed and could repeat chapter after chapter from memory.

Fowling Accident

The first fowling accident that occurred on Hirta during my time was on 12th August 1916. Ewen Gillies, who lived in No. 12 Main Street, was the only Islander that left Hirta bound to find a wife on the mainland. In this he was successful. So he came back to the Island with a very attractive young wife from Caolas, Scalpay, by the name of Margaret, who spoke the language of the Island, perfect Gaelic. They were married at Tarbert, Harris, by a Free Presbyterian minister in the summer of 1916.

The natives of the Island received her very graciously with open arms as if she was one of their own. I remember the couple on their arrival at Hirta pier were welcomed by well wishers and quite a number of the natives followed them to the groom's house. A reception was held the next day at which young and old sat down to a lovely meal to honour the newly wedded couple for the first time in the history of the Island. The missionary on the Island, Alexander MacKinnon, a native of the Isle of Skye, a man who had a great sense of humour, he acted on this occasion as a master of ceremony after he asked the blessing on the food. Young and old enjoyed a delicious dinner.

He told a story that I enjoyed immensely. I wrote it down and memorised it. An elder minister, who was for the third time a widower, got into conversation with one of his elders, to whom he mentioned his intention of marrying for the fourth time, 'Ay John,' said his reverence. 'This will be my fourth time', 'Just', said John slowly but moodily. 'I would like to have another, just to close my eyes when I'm leaving this world, you know', said the minister, 'What do you think of it John?' 'I weel,' said John humorously, 'I've only had two but I can tell ye, they've opened my eyes.'

In 1916 an accident occurred. Two able-bodied men lost their lives on the first day of the fulmar harvest, namely Ewen Gillies who married the mainland woman and John MacDonald who lived in No. 9 Main Street St Kilda, and was only married five weeks before this accident happened at the back of Connacher. It was a beautiful and warm summer day, they left home about 9 in the morning. It would take them approximately 46 minutes to arrive at the spot where they lost their lives. Both of these men were experienced cragsmen, they took 360 fulmars from that same spot, 12th August 1915. On that occasion I'm not certain whether it was MacDonald that harvested the 360 fulmars. I'm inclined to think that it was. I believe that I heard this discussed by John's father and mine. John's father was in his 80s when this happened.

It appears, arriving at the place, that Ewen tied the rope around his waist and so did John. Ewen descended over the cliff in a manner that a cragsman would do without fear of anything; this he did since he left school so he didn't think anything of it. Ewen was of heavy build weighing 200 lb, a gentle man by nature and was greatly respected by all. His quiet sense of humour, his gratitude for any service rendered, and his innate humility made him a firm favourite in his St Kilda home as elsewhere. He was a member of the St Kilda Church, the United Free Church of Scotland. The communion service that was held in the latter part of July on Friday, the *Ceist* day, when the presiding clergyman asked one of the brethren to present a text for discussion, Ewen rose up and presented the following text, John's Gospel chapter 9, verse 25; 'He answered and said, whether he be a sinner or no, I know not. One thing I know, that whereas I was blind, now I see.' Here it is in the language in which it was given that day; *'An sin fhreagair esan agus thubhairt e, Am peacach e chan aithne dhomh; air aon nì tha fhios agam: air dhomh bhi dall, gu bheil mi nis a' faicinn.'* As it is always customary, the one who presents the text is asked to close the Service with prayer. Ewen was a God fearing man and John was a God fearing man, but different natured. He was one who was a great favourite of the young people, he too was a member of the church.

John only weighed about 165 lb and, seeing that he didn't take the precautions he should have, when Ewen lost his balance and fell over the precipices he dragged John with him. If he had been anchored to the strong peg that was there this could have held both of them. Ewen's body was recovered on a ledge but John's body was never located. John's wife and Ewen's wife left their home round about 1 p.m., carrying their lunch and also to give a hand in carrying the fulmars home at 2 p.m. The women detected that something was wrong. John's wife Christene climbed the mountain and came to the lookout on Mullach Mhòr, her own brother happened to be on duty at the time, John. So he telephoned to the Naval station that Ewen and John were missing, so the alarm was sounded. Some of the Islanders had returned home, others were still away in the cliffs. Next day the body of Ewen was discovered. After the funeral, which approximately took three days, the Islanders returned to harvest their winter delicacy; it had to be done in order to survive.

During my lifetime, that was the only accident that occurred harvesting the fulmar. After this accident occurred I did notice this, that each rope was tested and where there was a pegged one on the top of the cliff, the man on top was anchored to it. John took a great interest in the young folks, teaching us various kinds of games to play. Hide and seek was one of these games and I remember the youngsters certainly loved it. The young folks of the Island felt the sense of a great loss of a personal friend. The friendship that he gave and the impressions he left were treasured by the youngsters of Hirta. His young wife returned home to her father's house, who was Finlay MacQueen who lived at No. 2 Main Street, St Kilda. She died of a broken heart four months after her husband's death. At Ewen's funeral the missionary Alexander MacKinnon presided, announcing the 103rd psalm, verses 14, 15 and 16; 'For He knoweth our frame: He remembereth that we are dust', finishing with the verse, 'For the wind passeth over and it is gone.' The 14th verse in Gaelic: *'Oir 's aithne dhàsan agus 's leìr ar cruth 's ar dealbh gu ceart, gur duslach talmhainn sinn air fad is cuimhne leis gu beachd.'* Our precentor William MacDonald, to the tune Dundee, was indeed very impressive. MacDonald was a born precentor and on account of his tenor voice, added so much to the worship.

[*The Gaelic Precentor*]

It would be only fitting that a word might be said about the Gaelic precentor; Gaelic worship is not complete without the precentor and the singing. The position of the precentor goes back to a time in Scotland when, following the Scottish Reformation, the use of musical instruments such as piano or organ were not allowed in any of the churches, with the result that some method of unaccompanied singing, such as the precentor could be placed in the category of a song leader, who intoned the psalm's verses, one by one. After a line thus presented, the congregation sang it.

I happened to be in Stornoway, summer of 1966 and I attended the Free Church on a Monday evening, which was the last service of the communions or I should say Monday was a thanksgiving day. A final service of thanksgiving was held after which the worshippers turned their faces homeward with happy memories of communion week. On that occasion the precentor precenting the lines and a congregation present of 800 singing the 72nd psalm to the tune of Stornoway, and all singing. May I say this, that the singing was very impressive.

The St Kilda thanksgiving service on Monday completing the service of the sacrament closed also with the 72nd psalm, also to the tune Stornoway. The missionary who was responsible for the Islands education used Friday afternoon from half past three to four teaching us the psalm tunes. He taught us Stornoway, Bangor, Coleshill, Dundee, Evan, Kilmarnock and Martyrdom. The precentor held a respected position in the church. The precentor's pulpit, which usually stood at the foot of the pulpit, I have no hesitation to say was second in dignity only to the minister's pulpit. I'm glad that the Island missionary taught the St Kilda scholars the psalm tunes. I found this very valuable during my ministry in Scotland and in Canada and I was glad that I was able to precent.

[*The First Death Recorded that Occurred on Boreray*]

Boreray is an Island 4 miles east of Hirta. This Island was famous for raising sheep. Every Islander had some sheep on Boreray with the exception of a couple of families that hadn't any. My neighbour to the west of us had not any, widow MacQueen No. 11 Main Street. As long as I can remember I can recall my mother preparing for this expedition weeks ahead baking, washing cloth and setting aside this article for the big box that my brother used to take to Boreray. As a general rule they spent a week on the island shearing the sheep.

There were three underground dwellings on Boreray: one belonging to the Gillies, the middle one to the MacDonalds and the third one to the Fergusons. The Gillies dwelling accommodated our family, John No. 15 Main Street, brother Donald living in No. 13 Main Street, our neighbour Donald Gillies living at No. 14 Main Street and his brother Neil living at No. 7 Main Street. They had to take with them dry straw. The straw was used for bedding.

[*Peat*]

The custom was to secure this on the Island of Boreray. The first chore was to cut peats and the last chore to see that it was placed in the *cleits* that were built for that purpose so when the Islanders returned to Boreray for sheep shearing they were certain that the peats were there ready to burn. This custom proved to be very successful, the peat never failed them. They took with them potatoes and fish. But on arriving on Boreray they killed a sheep and this sheep was shared between three dwellings. Puffin was at their door so there was no problem catching the puffin. They had their dogs with them so they were away as far as fresh meat and fowl was concerned.

They had a method of communicating with the inhabitants of the Island of Hirta. Certain spots were assigned a little distance from the three underground dwellings. A certain spot on Boreray if the turf was removed, which made a fairly large size of a black patch in this certain area, meant that death took place on the Island of Boreray. Another spot for sickness, and the third spot was when the turf was removed and a black patch was seen indicated that their work was completed, and now they want off.

My father saw to it that I went to the spot that I could see the Island of Boreray clearly every day and I can recall him saying wait until you see the sunshine shining on Boreray. I had a telescope so this particular morning I did notice the black patch when the turf was removed. The spot indicated that death had taken place on the Island of Boreray. He himself used to go until John, the second oldest of the family, arrived at the age of 20. So he took his place. Immediately five men set out in one of the Island boats. The day was ideal: a little breeze from the west which helped the boat on its way, when the sail was lifted the wind favourable. The great question in the mind of the women and men on Hirta: who was the victim? Something that was very hard to guess on account of when the men left for Boreray they were all in the best of health. Every person on the Island that was able to move on to the jetty was waiting for the boat's return with the remains and also the men with their dogs returned and never again did the St Kildians go on an expedition to stay on the Island. That was the final trip.

The death that took place was our neighbour Donald Gillies, a young man of 36 years of age. His father was Finlay Gillies, who lived at No. 7 Main Street. Donald was married to Finlay MacQueen's oldest daughter, who lived at No. 2 Main Street, Annie. He had four of a family: Mary, Christene, Rachel and Flora. Christene, who was only six years of age, accompanied her father to the Island of Boreray on this sad trip. This is the first time that such a young girl was included in what was the last expedition to the Island of Boreray. The reason for her going still remains a mystery. However, it was a sad trip for her to see her father, who loved her dearly, passing on to his eternal reward. The Islanders maintain that he died of appendicitis and every indication points in that direction on account of its suddenness. One could never have better neighbours than this family. Unfortunately medical aid wasn't available; if anyone took sick the St Kildians always applied a poultice made of oatmeal or a dose of castor oil or salts.

Donald, as he was known to us, established a home on the Island of Hirta which he was greatly proud of: one of kindness, loyalty and friendship, where father and mother had a great respect for one another, where the simplest food is good enough for kings because it is earned, where money is not so important as loving kindness and where even the tea kettle sings for happiness. That is the type of home that Donald and his wife Annie established on the Island of Hirta. His short life bears witness to the fact that he was greatly respected as a man who was always ready to help the aged, the sick and the needy. He was a Christian gentleman in every sense of the word so, for him as a Christian, death was just a translation from an unfriendly world to a world where our best friend awaits us. It is just a carriage that takes us from a land of sorrow and heartbreak to a land where God wipes away every tear. A neighbour and friend who knew him intimately for a few years truthfully speaks of him as a good, kind and honest man, a Nathanael without guile. I mentioned the fulmar accident.

Two Fatal Fishing Accidents

The first and only fishing accident that occurred on the Island of Hirta during my sojourn there was round 1st October 1906 and my first year at school. One of the senior pupils asked permission from the teacher Mrs MacLachlan if he would be permitted to leave early in the afternoon in order to join his two brothers Donald and Neil who were going to fish to Oiseval. It was Norman Gillies, who was fifteen years of age. There were also in the party two more, Neil Ferguson and Norman MacKinnon. Permission was granted. Mrs MacKinnon, 'Before your departure we shall have our closing hymn, Norman, and you suggest one', and he did, 'God be with you until we meet again'.

After the hymn, Norman left the school with a big smile on his face. Norman was very friendly and a favourite of one and all and none of us ever thought that would be the last time we would ever see that happy smile. I often think what a ready smile means to the individual; a smile creates happiness in the home, fosters goodwill in business, and is the counter sign of friendship. It brings rest for the weary, cheer to the discouraged and sunshine to the sad. Norman was blessed with this cheery smile. That meant a great deal to us pupils. He was always ready to help with our lessons and also he was our favourite on the playfield. He joined the party arriving at the fishing spot: everything went well, caught a number of fish called bream. As he got up to go home he lost his balance and fell into the sea. The party heard the splash but here none of the party could swim; they threw their fishing rods and ropes to no avail. The alarm was sounded and a boat launched but it was too late. The weather was calm if only a swimmer was available. On our return to school on Thursday, I remember the missionary Mr Peter MacLachlan conducting a memorial service the first thing in the morning, concluding this service by all the scholars repeating the Lord's Prayer together. The school was closed for three days.

I remember often accompanying my father to Ruaval on fishing trips. Arriving at the fishing spot, my father's first chore was to see that I was secured: rope tied to a peg and also tied around my waist. Fishing was excellent most of the time. There was another outstanding day in May 1918; a beautiful day, sea calm and on account of this the Islanders took advantage of it and crossed the four miles to the Island of Boreray seeking fulmar and puffins. So the Island was deserted of all the able bodied men with the exception of two brothers, Norman and John MacQueen. Norman was married and lived at No. 11 Main Street, Hirta. His brother lived at No. 10 Main Street. These brothers had some business to transact on the Dun in reference to lambs that were placed on the Dun in October.

William MacDonald, who was our precentor and also had the largest family on the Island, lived at No. 3 Main Street. He was the owner of a boat which by appearance was a canoe. This was the first of its kind that was ever seen on St Kilda. The St Kildians were accustomed to flat bottom boats and a flat bottom boat was hard to capsize. St Kildians were excellent sea men. I can recall my father discussing his plans for the day. He was planning on visiting the Dun also, but he planned to go at low tide from Ruaval to Dun. This could be done because there was a long chain on the Dun, anchored on top, and the bottom of the chain was very close to the water. That day was ideal to visit the Dun in that manner on account of the spring low tide. However for some reason or another mother persuaded him to join the party that was going over in this canoe or boat as you may call it and this he did.

As far as my opinion is concerned, I believe in the first place that they overloaded this canoe full of three big men. I am sure each of them would weight 200 lb, the two brothers would weigh in the neighbourhood of 165 lb each and none of them were accustomed to this type of boat. The Village Bay was like a pond, not even a ripple on the water, very calm. Arriving at the Dun the two brothers were preparing to go ashore and as customary they had tied the rope around their waist so they were attached to one another arriving at the landing spot, and as one of the brothers was preparing to jump ashore, the canoe capsized and threw them all into the water. Neil MacKinnon happened to have an oar in his hand and he clung to it. Donald MacDonald, Lachlan's father, had another oar and he also clung to it but apparently he was unfortunate to have wooden clogs on, with the result that the wooden clogs kept his head underwater, and he drowned. No doubt it was the clogs that he was wearing that was the cause of it.

Father clung to the canoe. He had a powerful voice that could be heard at a considerable distance, which in this case saved his life. I would say that the distance would be at least 2 miles yet mother heard his voice calling for help immediately. She informed Angus Gillies who lived at No. 6 Main Street, and my grandfather Donald Ferguson and both of them made a bee line to the school house. All the able boys were recruited, got hold of Angus's boat, lifted it bodily and launched it below the factor's storehouse. Arriving at the Dun they rescued Neil MacKinnon first, Donald MacDonald and my father last, so Donald MacDonald and the two MacQueen brother were lost. The body of Donald MacDonald was discovered and I recall the boat landing at the pier with two survivors and the remains of Donald MacDonald. MacDonald's body was carried by Angus Gillies to MacDonald's home, No. 16 Main Street, St Kilda. I remember an Aberdeen trawler trawled at the Dun and near the spot the MacQueen's boys were drowned. This effort was to no avail; their bodies were never recovered.

[*My Father*]

He was an elder and a good one at that. He was not the owner of many books but those he possessed he read: the works of Boston, Pilgrim's Progress, Rev. Robert MacCheyne and his Bible. His own soul was fed on strong meat and he was able to take out of his treasure things new and old. He had a powerful voice that could be heard at a considerable distance. Father in appearance was medium height, well built and of a ruddy countenance – in fact he had the appearance of a man that could endure hardness. The communion season on the Island on *ceist* days – he was never passed over, however large the number of available lay speakers. The people heard him gladly.

He was pre-eminently a man of prayer; he never left the barn without a prayer. When he finished feeding the cattle, he then would kneel in prayer. As a little boy I found myself with him on occasions like this. In prayer at times, when he was blessed with freedom of expression, it was noteworthy how aptly he employed the language of Scripture; every quotation was perfectly rendered and faultlessly appropriate. The gift of prayer was his in fuller measure than that of any man I have even listened to either in pulpit or pew. In 1926 he visited me in Glasgow; at that time I was in charge of a small mission on the south side on Eaglesham Street. This mission was under the supervision of Hope Street Free Church. During his stay with me, he conducted the service on Sunday evening in July, his last Sunday in the city before returning to his home in St Kilda. That particularly Sunday he spoke on the text John 3, verse 16: 'For God so loved the world that he gave his only begotten son, whosoever believeth in me should not perish.' There happened to be an elder present from the Free Church in Carloway, Lewis. Outside the mission hall that night this was the remark he made referring to father's prayer. He said 'I have heard many prayers but I never heard a prayer in my life like the one I heard tonight.' I thought that this was a great compliment that this saintly elder from Lewis paid father.

[*Donald MacDonald*]

In reference to our next door neighbour Donald MacDonald that lost his life by drowning, Lachlan's father, Donald MacDonald, was of medium height, of good appearance, and scrupulously neat in his habits and dress. According to the account I learned from his great friend Angus Gillies, who resided at No. 6 Main Street St Kilda, MacDonald feared the Lord from his youth up. It would appear that, like John the Baptist, he was filled with the Holy Ghost from his mother's womb. He was an earnest, active Christian and he was an excellent conversationalist. He was of a cheerful disposition; indeed, there was nothing gloomy about him. Young and old loved and respected him while he lived and mourned for him when he died. 'The righteous shall be in everlasting remembrance.' The mission that they were on that day was to see the progress of the lambs they had placed on the Dun in October and to examine if there was sufficient grass available for the stock to survive, a trip that ended in tragedy.

Miss MacCrimmon

During my days on the Island there were seventeen native houses occupied, one of these what we call a black house. One individual female lived in this type of dwelling, a Miss MacCrimmon. Apparently she simply refused to be moved from that type of dwelling; she was accustomed to it, and she had no desire for a change. She was offered the same type of dwellings the rest of the Islanders were enjoying but she simply refused so therefore she ended her day in the type of home she loved. The house was black both inside and out as she herself was with years of smoke. The fireplace was a hole in the roof with a large canopy coming down over the fire to draw the smoke up. The fire itself was placed on large stone slabs at floor level. There was an iron swey fixed somewhere in the centre of the canopy with a hook suspended to hang a pot or kettle to cook the food.

She was very interested in the church. I can recall myself and my younger brother accompanying father to her house. She was related to my father. My brother and I were a bit in awe of her, as we used to think she was like a witch. To convince us of such a thought, seeing an old fashioned broomstick by the fire, we were sure she must be. She was a kindly old soul and we were always treated to a piece of a scone which she produced from a tin. We thanked her and said we would eat it on the way home but I'm afraid the birds of the air got it as it reeked of smoke. She had only one big room, the bed in a corner, and the mattress was of straw. In the other end of this type of dwelling there was a stall that would accommodate a cow but she did not have one, but she did keep a few hens.

She loved her church. Margaret Ferguson who resided at No. 4 Main Street, who was also a spinster and very close to the age of Rachel MacCrimmon, used to call on Rachel on her way to church. This particular monthly meeting that was held at 11 a.m., Margaret forgot that Rachel MacCrimmon was waiting for her in order to accompany her to church. Apparently it must have dawned on her that her friend Margaret had forgotten so she made for church. The missionary had just given out his text when Rachel entered the church. She had her walking stick and I remember her lifting her walking stick and pointing it in the direction of Margaret, with the Gaelic word 'get away'. The expression on her face indicated that she was a little disturbed, putting it mildly. However, after a day or two they were both friends again and I do not believe that this instant happened again.

On another occasion I remember the missionary's sermon was based on John's Gospel chapter 14 where it says 'Let not your heart be troubled, ye believe in God. Believe also in me. In my Father's house are many mansions, if it were not so I would have told you. I go to prepare a place for you.' As she was sitting in the first seat as you enter the church, and as it was customary for the women to leave first, she would be among the first to leave the church. This occurred on a Sabbath evening. Here she stood, her back to the stone wall opposite the door of the church, and addressing every worshipper as he passed by. Her message was this: 'If you want to have a place in my Father's mansion above, believe in Him.' On this occasion she became a missionary.

Thinking of that instant today, I believe that, while things are arranged in this life so that we have no final knowledge of life after death, nevertheless we are given hints from time to time that are too strong to be ignored or brush aside and I fully believe that Mrs R. MacCrimmon on that day had a premonition that this was her last Sunday at church, as it turned out to be. Her neighbour was Neil MacKinnon, who never missed every morning going to her abode with a cup of tea. So this Monday morning with the tea cup in his hand he noticed that the lamp was still burning. On entering he found Rachel lying on top of the bed, her eyes closed as if she was asleep. Rachel passed on to the home of many mansions she was repeating to all the worshippers. Her passing was the last Islander who lived in, as it was commonly called, a black house. So on this particular Monday one of the old landmarks of Hirta was removed. I heard a neighbour, who knew her intimately for many years, truthfully speaking of her as a good, kind and honest woman; a Nathanael without a guile.

[*Neil MacKinnon*]

Referring to her neighbour, who certainly was a neighbour and a real Samaritan, Neil MacKinnon who resided at No. 1 Main Street, he was the other survivor at the Dun tragedy when the two brothers MacQueen were lost and Donald MacDonald drowned, but his body was discovered. Neil was of medium height and of good appearance. He was more widely known as a man of piety than as a speaker, although he was by no means destitute of the gift of speech. I remember hearing the missionary that visited Neil on his deathbed affirm that the effect of his visit to the dying Christian left a great impression with him. It was not so much the word that was spoken as the matter of utterance that made so profound an impression upon the missionary. It certainly could be said of him, well done good and faithful servant thou wert faithful in few things enter into the joy of thy Lord.

[*Duncan and Farquar Mhòr*]

As youngsters we were looking for stories. One outstanding story connected with St Kilda that I heard often by my father and grandfather tells of two brothers Duncan and Farquar Mhòr who were accused of sheep stealing. These men apparently were natives of the Isle of Lewis. These men were known throughout the Highlands, especially for their great strength and courage. They visited part of Uist, Harris and also the Isle of Skye in search of sheep and anything of value that they could lay their hands on. These two brothers made their way to St Kilda and for quite a number of days they enjoyed the hospitality of the Islanders but on the evening of the sixth day Duncan, who had climbed up to the top of Oiseval, suddenly started crying out that he could see warships between Hirta and Boreray. The distance between Hirta and Boreray is 4 miles. Farquar, who stayed with the inhabitants, advised the population to take shelter in the temple. The natives did not take much coaching in doing this very thing because they were terrified. Farquar got all the St Kildians excited and in those days it would take very little to do that.

The moment they got all the St Kildians inside the temple, the two robbers blocked the entrance and laid whatever wood, grass, straw and heather against the outside walls. Thus they were successful in setting fire to the temple and burned the occupants alive. As far as they were concerned, they thought that they destroyed every one on the Island. However, they were mistaken in their count. One elderly woman, who had been over at Glean Mhòr, had not heard Duncan's warning. On her way back to the village she detected a strange smell, not unlike the smell of burning flesh, which she accurately judged to be a sign that all was not well. She had the sense of immediately hiding herself in a cave on Ruaval; the cave is facing east. Thus she could see the moment the steward's boat entered Village Bay and also from this cave she had a good view of the homes on the Island and she was also in a position to watch the movements of those two killers. When darkness came she crept down into the empty village. While the two murderers slept she took what food she could find and returned to the cave.

For a considerable time the elderly woman managed to survive, hiding by day and stealing food by night without being found out. One day the steward's boat appeared on the horizon for the annual visit to collect the rent. Duncan and Farquar went down to the shore to meet him, ready to present to the rent collector and the captain of the boat what had happened to the Islanders. They had no doubt in their minds that it would be accepted without question. They must have got the surprise of their lives when they noticed the elderly woman making for the shore to meet the rent collector and the captain of the boat. The moment she saw the ship anchored she left the cave that had been a home for several months. The words of the elderly lady were 'It's come, my God', in the language she was using, the Gaelic *'Thàinig mo Dhia, thàinig mo Dhia'*, who was thrilled when she saw the boat on the horizon and her cave was an ideal spot to see the ship. I visited the cave on several occasions and also had the privilege of showing it to tourists. The lady told her story to the rent collector and captain. Her story was accepted without question.

The rent collector, or steward as he was called, at once ordered Duncan and Farquar to be seized. They were taken and marooned on Soay, where it was thought they would not survive long without a fire, but as the steward and his men were leaving, they overheard Duncan asking Farquar if he had got the flint and tinder safe. Having this detail the steward decided to leave Duncan on Soay and moved his brother to Stac an Armin, but Farquar refused to stay and swam after the boat pleading for mercy until he drowned on Soay. Duncan managed to live a little longer. I have seen the cave which still bears his name. As far as the story goes, the steward took the elderly lady away from the Island and for a time the Island was deserted. No one seemed to know what really became of the only survivor.

[*Stories on St Kilda*]

At times I was told a fairy story at bedtime: two St Kildians, one Neil MacDonald and Donald MacKinnon, were gathering peats on *Glean Mhòr.* They came to a green knoll and they heard a strange noise. On hearing this they stood silent for a few minutes and to their great surprise a door opened a few yards away from a fairy woman, very attractively dressed in a green garment. She confronted the men and made a generous offer to each one: a bowl of milk. It took them by surprise. Nevertheless one of the men, Neil MacDonald, accepted her generous offer but before drinking it he crossed himself in the name of the Father, Son and Holy Ghost. The fairy did not consider it very polite so apparently withdrew her offer and disappeared into the knoll.

On another occasion, a certain mother was visited by two fairy women clad in green. Seeing the child in her arms they robbed her of power of speech, but she heard the fairies discuss together the gift of fluency of tongue, which they were about to bestow on the child. It was said that this particular person was given the ability to out talk twenty people without feeling tired.

Bible stories were the prominent ones. The story of Joseph and the coat of many colours: the pit and selling him to the Ishmaelites, third part Joseph in prison, fourth part the dream and the fifth the restoration of Joseph to the high post of Governor of Egypt. The tales of the covenanters, especially Margaret Wilson, the martyr of the Solway sand, tied to the stake in the channel of the sea from which the waves retired. At low water was fixed a stake, whither between two ruffian soldiers the helpless girl was led and her arms bound to her body with ropes. In the meantime, she was again promised her life and freedom if she would take the test. 'Not by any means. I trust in my God and I know that He will not forsake me.' It seems to me that mother placed emphasis on her last words as they always remained with me. 'Farewell my friend. Farewell my enemies – thou sun and thou earth, farewell. Come, ye waters; why come ye so slowly, come and waft my soul to the bosom of my God.' This story I never forgot.

I can recall on another occasion a bunch of boys were playing in a certain field and I was one of them. One of the church members told us to leave that field, that we shouldn't play there. One of the boys uttered a swear word. This instant we arrived at our home after receiving a tongue lashing. The story that night was taken from the second book of Kings, chapter 2, commencing with the story from verse 19, 'And the men of the city said unto Elisha, Behold, I pray thee, the situation of this city is pleasant, as my Lord seeth; but the water is naught, and the ground barren. And he said, Bring me a new cruse, and put salt therein. And they brought it to him. And he went forth unto the spring of the waters, and cast the salt in there, and said, Thus saith the Lord, I have healed these waters; there shall not be from thence any more death or barren land. So the waters were healed unto this day, according to the saying of Elisha which he spake. And he went up from thence unto Bethel and as he was going up by the way there came forth little children out of the city, and mocked him, and said unto him, Go up you bald head, go up, thou bald head. And he turned back, and looked on them, and cursed them in the name of the Lord. And there came forth two she-bears out of the wood and tare forty and two children of them and he went from thence to mount Carmel, and from thence he returned to Samaria.' And may I say that I was terrified. I couldn't get over the two she-bears coming out of the woods; believe me, that instant taught me a lesson.

After that I was careful that a swear word was not uttered in the presence of an elderly person. That bedtime story taught me to be more polite in the future. These were the type of bedtime stories I was accustomed to in my youth. The vow that my parents took when I was baptised, do you promise to bring up this child in the nurture and [admonition] of the Lord. When they said, 'we do' they meant it and lived it. The story of Daniel and the lion's den was another story I was often told at bedtime.

[*The Gillies Family of No. 6 Main Street, St Kilda*]

At the age of 16 in the year 1917 the occupant of No. 6 Main Street took sick. He was unable to carry out the various chores in order to keep the home fire burning so I was responsible to see that he had sufficient peat at hand to keep the fire burning. His wife was no help to him; as a matter of fact, she was mentally ill. On one occasion Dr Shearer visited the Island; this doctor made one visit a year.

On this particular visit I was urgently summoned to No. 6 Main Street and acted as an interpreter; Dr Shearer did not speak Gaelic and mostly all his patients on the Island were Gaelic speaking. Mrs Gillies had a pain in her shoulders, her left foot was sore and also she was complaining that she had no appetite. She never left the house; she spent more time in bed than sitting up. She was the only woman on the Island that did not attend church and the only woman during my sojourn on the Island that smoked. She had a grey clay pipe and she smoked the strongest tobacco on the market, called Black Twist.

Her husband Angus, who was indeed a God fearing man, did everything in his power to please her. This she did not appreciate. I often heard her calling him a liar and accusing him of not helping her. I have often witnessed food beside her bed that he placed there but the moment she found that he had gone to church she would take advantage of this and helped herself to any food she could lay her hands on. They had one son and he died at the early age of 19. According to what I have learnt from his father and other Islanders this lad feared the Lord from his youth. When he was of age to attend school he was known frequently to part with his playmates and go aside to pray. The spirit of devotion remained with him through his short life.

As a matter of fact the Lord revealed to him the hour of his departure from this world. He tried to comfort his father and mother the best way he could. He asked them not to mourn for him but to go on living normally. This was the message to his parents and to all the Islanders: 'I want you my loved ones on earth to carry on the torch of life. I'll be waiting for you all in that land that is fairer than day.' The smile of welcome was exceedingly attractive indeed according to all reports. Indeed there was nothing gloomy or sad about him; young and old loved and respected him while he lived, and mourned for him when he died: 'The righteous shall be in lasting remembrance.'

Dying at the early age of 20, this might have been the cause of his mother's mental illness. She took ill and to her bed immediately after his death. As to his father: 'His life', one said at his death, 'was a bright and unmistakable evidence of the grace of God in his heart'. He was well read and had a strong retentive memory. It was a rare treat to listen to him, always in Gaelic of course, either speaking on a passage of Scripture, when conducting a prayer meeting, or speaking at the fellowship meeting on *ceist* day at a communion season. Moreover, he was a power in the prayer meeting on Wednesday evening in the church. He filled the office of elder with great ability, dignity and grace for twenty-five years, and all through his life he was a tower of strength to the Christian church of his day.

Angus was different from the majority of Christians at that time in regard to his attitude towards the temperance question. This is something that the St Kildians did not need to worry about during my lifetime on the Island; I never heard or saw anyone under the influence of liquor. I saw my father and others taking a social drink on special occasions, such as New Year's Day. As far as the Islanders were concerned, whisky was considered a good gift from God for which all men were bound to give thanks. Angus Gillies, however, was for many years a total abstainer and until the end of his day.

My uncle Neil Ferguson and Angus's neighbour told me that Angus called at a friend's home, No. 8 Main Street, and the good lady of the house [Margaret MacKinnon] offered a glass of liquor. He shook his head saying, 'There has not a glass of liquor gone to my lips in twenty years.' Taking the glass away, she emptied the liquor into a mug remarking with more hospitality than sound logic. 'You can still say so.' 'No no Margret', he replied, 'It is all the same, what I will not take from a glass I will not take from a mug.'

[*Wool*]

The only weekday prayer meeting the Islanders miss is during the season of shearing the sheep. I believe the Islanders were the only ones shearing a sheep with a good pocket knife; this was the Islanders' way of doing it from time immemorial. I have witnessed them on Harris shearing the sheep but they used shears. This wool was washed. The black wool was kept apart from the white. One can notice on the Island big boulders of stone and on some of these stones crodal is found. A day or two each summer was set aside to scrape the crodal from these big stones. Then the big pot that was kept especially for this purpose was located. The first calm day a fire was lit outside and the pot was placed on the iron chain with a hook. All day that pot was kept boiling, crodal and wool mixed together. This wool was washed and made ready for the carding.

The same method was used for the indigo blue. A night would be set apart to card this wool and mix the dyed wool with the white. So we used to produce four rolls of tweed crodal coloured red, two rolls of the indigo blue and three rolls of black and white. Each roll of tweed in length was 33 yards and in width 28 inches. During my day, the price was 3 shillings and six pence a yard.

[*Supplies to the Island*]

My uncle who was a tweed merchant in Glasgow bought all the tweed from the Islanders. He was responsible to see that the winter supply was landed on the Island during the summer month such as the necessities of life: flour, sugar, tea, shoes and salt. The gloves, sheepskins, and the odd piece of tweed that the Islanders sold to tourists during the summer month was ready cash, and they kept this in order to use it during the winter month. Trawlers from Aberdeen, Hull, Grimsby and Fleetwood visited the Island regularly and went out of their way to supply the Islanders with groceries, those who smoked with tobacco and also a certain amount would be set aside for Sunday collection. The amount I was given each Sunday was a penny for each service and usually two services on Sunday 11 a.m. and 6 p.m.

My grandfather Donald Ferguson, who was the elder in the Kirk, during my day used to go around once a year and collected from each family as much as they could afford to give to the sustentation fund of the United Free Church of Scotland. This sum that was collected was sent to the headquarters of the said church, which was the capital of Scotland, Edinburgh, once a year. This custom is still carried on in the Highlands of Scotland in Lewis, Uist and Harris; so the inhabitants of St Kilda did not differ from any other parts of the Highlands.

[*Old Age Pension*]

David Lloyd George, premier of Great Britain, introduced the old age pension of seven shillings and six pence a week. To my knowledge the following individuals qualified for this old age security: Angus Gillies, Donald Ferguson, Mrs Angus Gillies, John MacDonald, Margaret MacKinnon and Rachel MacCrimmon and this indeed was a Godsend to these people. The names mentioned had arrived at the age that they were unable to provide for themselves the necessary chores that were essential in order to keep the home fires burning. These individuals depended on their neighbours and friends to help in various directions: cutting peats on the hills, carrying it to their homes, looking after their sheep on the hills and planting their garden such as potatoes and vegetables. These people felt more comfortable on account of the old age pension which placed them in an independent category. Now they were able to offer a few shillings to those who were their helpers.

I received this from Angus Gillies for carrying his peats to his home, and other little chores such as cutting his grass, and seeing it secured into the *cleit* for the winter. I remember at the end of December 1916 that I received from Angus the amount of 2 pounds. I used to keep it and during the summer month buy candies, biscuits and shortbread. *Dunara Castle*, which made a fortnightly visit to the Island, used to have a canteen that one could purchase the articles mentioned. This was certainly a big day in my young life and other youngsters my age.

[*My First Job*]

I remember my first job that I was really hired on a day's pay, which was 2 shillings and sixpence a day. The missionary on the Island in the year 1917, Mr Alexander MacKinnon, hired me for the purpose of making his hay. My father provided me with a scythe so towards the end of August I commenced my first job. In those days, at the age of 16 I did not think that any job was hard. However, my father supervised the haying and the scholars of the day helped me to gather it, place a big bulk of it on the barn's loft and the rest was secured and placed in the *cleits* adjacent to the manse. It took me approximately five weeks and I still remember that my remuneration amounted to five pounds. However that five pounds went to help the home. As youngsters we were taught to be good cragsmen. When we arrived at manhood the cliffs became naturally to me, as a matter of fact it became a part of my life.

[*Weaving*]

As a youngster I was also taught weaving. The home-made loom would be set up in the kitchen around the first of February for teaching how to become an expert weaver. The first piece placed in the loom would be a blanket and this was not for sale. So as beginner you were given the opportunity to show your skill, with father of course as a supervisor. This is how I was taught to become a weaver and if one intended to settle on the Island, weaving was a must. The men of the Island were all weavers; the spinning was entirely women's work. Men would card or tease the wool.

[*Lachlan MacDonald*]

A few years before the evacuation, I learnt with great satisfaction that Lachlan MacDonald who lived with his mother at No. 16 Main Street took up spinning. He and his mother lived alone. His older brothers Ewen, Angus and Donald had left the Island and the three brothers were employed in Yarrows Shipyard in Partick, Glasgow, and established homes of their own in that city. So Lachlan, the youngest of the family, was his mother's only support. She suffered with arthritis which left her unable to spin as she used to. So Lachlan became the first Islander to become an expert at the spinning wheel. He had one sister married to Neil Gillies, son of Finlay Gillies, and lived at No. 7 Main Street, St Kilda. Neil died in an Oban Hospital, a comparatively young man, and left the widow with two children and also her father-in-law, Finlay Gillies. Lachlan also lost a sister who died as a young girl who was attending school at the time of her passing; the reason [for her death] unknown. There was no nurse on the Island at the time. This attractive young girl was called Rachel, a young girl who was well liked by all.

So Lachlan was the youngest and not only looked after his mother but as a young man he helped the widow and the aged on the Island. Young men on the Island were very scarce before the evacuation of the Island in 1930 so Lachlan was in great demand and called on by his neighbours to do this and that for them. His own sister was a widow and her father-in-law Finlay was well over seventy. So Lachlan had to attend to their sheep on the hills and had to go at the time of harvesting the fulmars for them. So without a shadow of doubt Lachlan was overworked on account of so few men capable of doing the work that was so essential for their survival on the Island; it takes youth and strength. When one takes into account that there was not a single horse on the Island, therefore tilling the land was by a spade. So much barley was sowed every year. The spade had to be used to plant potatoes.

So human power was doing the work that a horse ought to do. In other parts of the Highlands, horses were used for ploughing the fields and also to carry home the peats. Horses could have done that same type of work on St Kilda, but for some reason or another no one had one. A horse would have been a very valuable animal on the Island, especially three years before the evacuation on account of the scarcity of human power.

[*Funerals on St Kilda*]

I have seen in a book written on St Kilda the writer goes on describing the method the Islanders used in burying the dead. What happened a hundred years before my time I'm not certain, but during my stay on the Island and from what I witnessed, the corpse was dressed in a white shroud and the face covered with a white handkerchief. In the reference to the red cloth wrapped around the corpse, this never happened during my day. The Islanders followed the teaching of Christ and I believe that the idea of the shroud came into being as described in the Gospel according to St Luke chapter 23 from verse 50: 'There was a man named Joseph a counsellor: and he was a good man, and a just. This man approached Pilate who was the Governor and begged the body of Jesus. This permission was granted and he took it down and wrapped in linen and laid it in a sepulchre that was hewn in stone, wherein never man before was laid.' The women were the first visitors at the tomb of Jesus and discovered the empty tomb. The only thing they discovered in the tomb was the shroud folded neatly at one end of the tomb and the handkerchief also that covered the Saviour's face neatly folded beside the shroud.

So the St Kildians followed this as closely as they could, for this type of dressing the corpse that I attended. Two or three men made the coffin in the factor's storehouse east of the manse. I certainly agree with Mary Cameron of the manse that they used a kettle of boiling water in order to help them to bend the wood they were using to make it to a shape of a shoulder. Not only did they receive boiling water but they were also supplied lunch from the occupants of the manse. I often heard the men speaking of the hospitable people in the manse. The first one I attended, the coffin was the colour of the wood. When this task was completed, the men carried the coffin on their shoulder to the house of mourning and the villagers gathered at the house. The missionary would read a chapter and at this particular one I can recall the chapter that Mr Alexander MacKinnon read was John's Gospel, chapter 14: 'Let not your heart be troubled; you believe in God, believe also in me. In my Father's house there are many mansions; if it were not so I would have told you. I go to prepare a place for you.' After this he would lead in prayer and after that the body was placed in the coffin and closed, as a matter of fact nailed.

That night the wake would take place. A sheep had been slaughtered, and tea, scones, bannock and mutton were served during the night. Remember that worship also took place. The next day the funeral would take place; worship at the house by the missionary. If the missionary was absent, an elder took his place. Worship ended and the coffin was removed from the house. Half of the window would be removed and the coffin was handed out through the window. Three poles were used to carry the coffin to its last resting place. Six people acted as pall bearers and carried the coffin to the cemetery. The villagers young and old walked behind the coffin. The walk would take approximately twenty minutes and, arriving at the grave, a prayer was offered and the coffin was lowered into the grave. The men that were present would immediately fill the grave. The villagers the next day returned to their normal tasks and school reopened that was closed for three days during this death.

Early in 1918, the custom of killing a sheep for a wake was abandoned. The Islanders were directed to read the 127th psalm and the second verse, *'Dhuibh 's dìomhain bhi ri mocheirigh, san oidhch ri caithris bhuain, bhi g' itheadh arain bròin; mar sin, dha sheircean bheir e suain.'* The English interpretation reads as follows: 'It is vain for you to rise up early, to sit up late, to eat the bread of sorrows; for so He giveth his beloved sleep.'

The last funeral I attended, the missionary was Mr Cameron. Death took place and the coffin was made in the same manner as the one I have already described with the exception that this time they varnished the casket they had made. The wake vanished and relatives remained with the mourners until after the funeral. School closed for the same number of days, three, and also all the Islanders were idle for three days.

Malcolm MacDonald who lived at No. 8 Main Street left St

Kilda shortly after the First World War. He had various jobs but his last one was in one of London, England's, attractive hotels. His sister Mary who lives in Melbourne, Australia, whom I visited in 1974, was telling me that Malcolm was very disappointed when he heard that the St Kildians were leaving the Island for good. Malcolm was contemplating retiring on the Island. He visited his native Island twice when he was on two working parties and every time he left he felt very lonesome. Malcolm passed away about a year ago. His last wish was that his ashes be buried in the cemetery on St Kilda. I'm delighted to report that this took place in September 1979. This is the first burial of this nature that ever took place in the St Kilda cemetery. Thanks to the British Government for arranging this. During my time on the Island the women were not left to dress the corpse; that task belonged to the family. I never saw what one of the writers of a book on St Kilda describes regarding blanket material used as a shroud. However, if this took place it was certainly before my day. And I never heard any of the old timers on the Island speaking about a blanket being used.

Arriving in Canada in 1927, my first appointment as a student missionary was in Cape Breton in the congregation of North River and North Shore in Victoria County. I arrived in that congregation late Saturday night and I stayed at the home of one of the elders, Dan A. MacLeod, North River, 14th May 1927. I preached twice on Sunday and on Monday I had to conduct a funeral. I asked Mr MacLeod every conceivable question I could think of as to the custom of conducting a funeral so I thought I had covered everything re a funeral service. The service was conducted from the house. The house was crowded and people were outside. As I entered the house and was directed to the living room where the coffin was, to my amazement here was a man in a coffin with an old fashioned English collar on and a bow tie. To be introduced to such a sight that I never saw nor expected to see, a man being buried in his best suit, the thought that struck me was this, the elderly gentleman dressed and nowhere to go. So 100 years before my day they might have used a blanket in my native Island to bury the dead. This gentleman that I buried was a Highlander that hailed from Harris in the Highlands of Scotland and this funeral service was conducted in the Gaelic language.

[*Mail Service to St Kilda*]

In reference to the mail service to the Island during the summer month beginning May to August. The two tourist steamers, the SS *Dunra Castle* and the *SS Hebrides*, sailed from Glasgow every fortnight on a ten day cruise carrying thirty-five passengers who paid £10 for the trip which included everything. These vessels called at Islay, Portaskie [*sic*], Oban, Tobermory, Coll, Tiree, Castlebay, Lochmaddy and St Kilda. The *Hebrides* landed at St Kilda on a Thursday and the *Dunra Castle* arrived at St Kilda on a Saturday afternoon, calling at the ports I have mentioned. On their return from St Kilda, they called at Obbe, Tarbet, Scalpay, Dunvegan and Oban, arriving back in Glasgow at the end of their ten days. In addition to passengers, these ships carried cargo and these ships were also fitted out to carry livestock. So during summer month one could depend on receiving mail regularly.

My uncle Neil Ferguson was elected postmaster in 1906. The minister on the Island was looking after the mail until my uncle was appointed at the end of May of the above noted year. My uncle built a one-room building adjacent to his home. He had in big print a sign 'St Kilda post office' placed above the door. He carried the mail on his back to the jetty and ferried out in a small boat to the steamers. The mail received, he used to deliver letters and parcels to each home. Before he took over, the Islanders used to go to the factor's house and collect their mail; the minister who was postmaster of the Island used the factor's house as a post office. Stamps were available at the post office and also postal orders.

Physically, Neil Ferguson was of medium height, of good appearance and very neat in his habits and dress. He had a fair English education and an excellent command of the Gaelic – his mother tongue. He was the one that conducted the services on Sunday on Boreray. Weather permitting, these services were held in the open air, if wet they were held in the largest underground dwelling, which was No. 1, belonging to the Gillies. As a postmaster he was often called upon to write letters for those who did not speak English: business letters at times, such as writing their requirements for the winter months such as flour, tea, sugar and shoes, and at other times letters to relatives. He was the only one of the natives that was on the pay roll all year round. He was married to Finlay MacQueen's sister, Finlay the famous cragsman, and lived at No. 2 Main Street.

Neil had three sons: Neil, Donald and John. Neil the oldest remained on the croft with his parents and attended especially to the sheep. This family had the largest stock on Hirta, and also on the Island of Boreray. So this kept Neil junior in business at all times and he indeed was an expert at looking after sheep. He married Finlay MacQueen's oldest daughter, and the first bride to be married in a white dress, in the St Kilda Kirk in 1926. This was also the last wedding to take place on the Island. Her youngest brother Norman MacQueen was best man.

The MacLeods of Dunvegan, Skye, were the original owners of the Island group, and everyone lived in the Village Bay area on Hirta, the main Island. The MacLeods were the owners during my life on the Island. Since I left, it has changed hands several times. In 1934 Sir Reginald MacLeod, whose family had owned St Kilda for centuries, sold the Island group to the fifth Marquis of Bute [and Earl of Dumfries], who bequeathed it on his death to the National Trust for Scotland. In January 1946, New Years Day, I spent the day with my uncle, Alexander Ferguson, the first part of the day at his home in Old Kilpatrick, a suburb of Glasgow. The afternoon I recall spending two hours in Dumbarton, where he kept his boat. He loved boats and also he certainly loved the sea. He showed me his boat, which he was rightly proud of. He had sailed from the Clyde, calling at Islay, Oban, Lochaline, Tobermory, Coll, Tiree, Lochmaddy and St Kilda. He loved the Island of his birth. I remember him telling me on this occasion, that during the Second World War he found himself in Obbe, Harris. No one was allowed on the Island. So, as he said, 'I hired a boat and went to a small Island called Shillay and stood on a top of a mountain on that Island', where he saw St Kilda under a white cap of summer haze. He said to me, 'Donald, as you are no doubt familiar with the Story of Moses, [it was as] when he viewed the Promised Land from Pisgah Heights.'

[*The Various Jobs of Men and Women on St Kilda in Summer and Winter*]

The women of the Island were very busy during the winter months spinning. The men helped by carding the wool and getting it ready for the spinning wheel. The men of the Island were the weavers and in the summer the men undertook the difficult and hazardous task of egg and bird collecting on the soaring sea cliffs. Connachair on Hirta, which rises 1,397 feet from the sea and, according to the opinion of the historian, is Britain's tallest sea cliff. No one was permitted to visit the Island during the Second World War; nevertheless on top of Connachair, members of the National Trust for Scotland discovered a war plane was wrecked and was able to locate the make, and also according to record that four Australians that manned this plane lost their lives. I understand that a suitable memorial plaque has been placed in the church with their names on it, and their families have been notified. 'They shall grow not old as we that are left grow old, age shall not weary them nor the years condemn, at the going down of the sun and in the morning we will remember them.'

[*Soay and other Lesser Islands*]

In October 1919 I was on Soay after sheep. I lost a very valuable sheepdog. He caught the sheep but the sheep dragged the dog over the cliff. I felt badly about this, losing such a young valuable dog. Soay and Boreray are formidable, as are the nearby stacks of Stac Lee and Stac an Armin. On these and many other cliffs of the archipelago, I along with other men were lowered by ropes of horse hair to collect the birds and their eggs on the ledges over the sea. Once these had been collected in a box and slung around the shoulders, the climber relied entirely upon the ability of his comrades at the cliff top to haul him up to safety again by plaited horse hair ropes from St Kilda.

The wife and I visited Scotland in August 1977. We took a bus tour from Buchanan Street, Glasgow, to the Highlands visiting Inverness, Fort Augustus, Culloden Moor, Lewis and the Isle of Skye. We visited Dunvegan Castle; wasn't I surprised to see the plaited horse hair ropes preserved for show at Dunvegan Castle. I can truly say that these ropes were hereditary possessions and were very valuable to us Islanders. Though Stac Birroch, I heard my father say that it was approximately 236 feet high. This I considered the hardest reputed climb in the archipelago. I remember I and the following: Neil Ferguson Junior, Finlay MacDonald, Norman MacQueen, John MacDonald and Angus MacDonald, climbed to the very top in July 1920. We harvested fulmars and eggs; we used the long rod for snaring the fulmars. We found it harder descending than we did climbing carrying a load of eggs on your back. I remember throwing the birds into the sea and those that were manning the boat collected them.

[*Difficulties of Landing on St Kilda*]

During my days on the Island, I believe the greatest major difficulty was a lack of communication with the outside world. The only available landing place on the permanently inhabited Island of Hirta is at Village Bay, and then only if a swell from the south is not running into the Bay; south wind with a swell, no one is able to land. During my life on the Island I can recall the main boat SS *Hebrides* was unable to land on four occasions. The tourists aboard were greatly disappointed on account of not landing on Hirta; no one to blame but the Atlantic swell. The North Bay landing can be made in a case of emergency. Dr MacDonald who brought the pure Gospel to the Island was forced to make a landing at North Bay. Small boats from ships that were sunk by German submarines did land on North Bay. A crew from a Norwegian cargo steamer and a Danish freighter, they also made a landing at North Bay.

The Rev. Donald John Gillies's brother Neil and their mother, Annie (née Ferguson), often referred to on the island as 'Queen of St Kilda'

Interior of the school, Village, Hirta, St Kilda where Donald John Gillies received his schooling (Reproduced by kind permission of James Russell)

The village street of Hirta, showing No.15 Main Street, the birthplace and home of Rev. Donald John Gillies, at near left (Reproduced by kind permission of James Russell)

The church and manse, Hirta, St Kilda (© National Trust for Scotland. Licensor www.scran.ac.uk)

The interior of the church, showing the precentor's desk, the pews of the various families as described by the Rev. Donald John Gillies and the wall plaque with the names of the airmen killed in all Second World War air crashes on St Kilda (Reproduced by kind permission of James Russell)

Mrs Annie Gillies (Donald John Gillies's mother), St Kilda, 1930
(© National Museums Scotland. Licensor www.scran.ac.uk)

Neil Ferguson (Donald John Gillies's uncle) carrying a sack of wool from St Kilda, 1930 (© National Museums Scotland. Licensor www.scran.ac.uk)

Neil Ferguson taking the last post to the post office, St Kilda, 1930
(© National Museums Scotland. Licensor www.scran.ac.uk)

Visitors to the island haggle with Mrs Gillies for a pair of hand-knitted gloves
(© Newsquest (Herald & Times) Licensor www.scran.ac.uk)

Finlay MacQueen outside his house, No. 2 Main Street, 9 August 1938, when he spent the summer on the island with Neil and Mrs Gillies (© School of Scottish Studies. Licensor www.scran.ac.uk)

After the main evacuation of the island in 1930, Mrs Gillies, Neil Gillies and Finlay MacQueen spent the summer of 1938 on St Kilda: here they are pictured waiting for the SS *Hebrides* on the jetty, 8 August 1938 (© School of Scottish Studies. Licensor www.scran.ac.uk)

Donald John Gillies's older brother, also named Donald, and brother Neil Gillies in 1966, off St Kilda (© Scottish Life Archive. Licensor www.scran.ac.uk)

The Rev. Donald John Gillies visiting St Kilda, possibly in 1966

The Rev. Donald John Gillies standing beside the First World War gun on St Kilda in August 1980 (Reproduced by kind permission of Peggy Askew)

The Rev Donald John Gillies with a group of St Kildans revisiting the island in August 1980 for the rededication of the recently restored church on the 50th anniversary of the evacuation of the island: the three people on his left are his nieces Rachel and Catherine Gillies and his nephew Norman John Gillies (Reproduced by kind permission of Peggy Askew)

[*Factors which Caused the Evacuation*]

My first visit to my mother's home in Larachbeg was May 1937; this is in the Lochaline area. At this time I took upon myself to find out the reason that prompted them to leave the Island. The information I gathered from my brothers John and Donald: the Islanders in 1928 discovered the dwindling population was not being replaced and backed up by younger stronger men. So I gathered from my brothers that the St Kildian Parliament decided to enlist Government support to resettle the population of the Island on the mainland. Many of the very old inhabitants, brother Donald said, one of eighty-six, were not very enthusiastic to the idea of leaving, and of course this is understandable at such an age. The Government decided to help on one condition: that all the Islanders were agreeable and in readiness to make a fresh start somewhere on the mainland.

Apparently each family was offered a house in Lochaline, with land for grazing, cultivation and work for the men with the Forestry Commission guaranteed for 130 days a year [*The actual arrangement was a guaranteed minimum of 105 days* – ed]. And so, August 1930, the Islanders began in real earnest to leave the Island and begin a new life on the mainland. So the task of gathering the sheep commenced on Boreray first; this Island is about 4 miles from the main Island Hirta. They were able to gather close on 500 sheep from this Island and there were about 1,400 sheep already gathered on the Island of Hirta. The number in total was 1,805. I was told that the SS *Dunra Castle* made three trips to Oban to move these animals, according to the information I received from my brothers in 1937. They recalled that there were thirty-six people on Hirta in August 1930; of this total, six were over 65, twenty were between 21 and 65, and ten were under 21. There was a school up to the time of evacuation and, besides the population already mentioned, there was a nurse and a protestant missionary.

My brother Donald gave this account of the last days on the

Island; using his own words he said it was hectic: On Tuesday 26th August, the Government Sloop *Harebell* arrived at Oban from Fleetwood to standby for favourable weather to take Islanders off the Island. There was bad weather intermittently through late August, and the *Harebell* continued to wait at Oban. The journey from Oban to St Kilda would take approximately nine hours once conditions became favourable. The season was getting late. Then one morning the wind changed direction, and the water in Village Bay settled, ideal for loading. So the last day on the Island came at last, said my brother, most of us went down to the pier for the last time with our possessions, but he said some of the older folks were slower at coming down. They took a last look around. Mother was the last to leave the home I was born. I saw a picture of her locking the door of No. 15 Main Street for the last time and also in the same picture was the spinning wheel she loved outside the door.

This was the last article she carried from the home. A spinning wheel she loved, and used it often in her new home in Larachbeg in the area of Lochaline in Argyllshire. The church was a distance of 3 miles from home; this distance she walked every Sunday and walked back. Her place in the Kiel church was very seldom empty. She died at the age of 87 and she is buried in Kiel cemetery. She was back a couple of times, and enjoyed her visit immensely. I can truly say that mother was very content with her life and lot in Lochaline. She saw her brothers at least once a year: Alex in Glasgow and Donald who was a Free Church minister in Scalpay, Harris. In reference to my sister-in-law Christine, she also enjoyed the mainland life; nevertheless she said to me on several occasions, 'I don't wish to remember anything about the life I lived on the Island of St Kilda. I want to forget it. That life is certainly behind me and I do not even wish to go back for a visit.' She repeated to me that those that wish to go let them go, but that won't tell them of all our hardship long ago, and my brother Donald, her husband, said to me, 'I have never been back and I never wish to.'

[*Catherine and Rachel and their Visit Back to St Kilda*]

Quoting from the *Daily Express* on 7th July 1979, the two daughters of my brother Donald:

> two Scots sisters will step back half a century into the lost world of their childhood tomorrow. An army landing craft will ferry them to the remote Atlantic Island of St Kilda, which they last saw in August 1930. Catherine and Rachel [who are my two nieces – DJG] were among the last of 16 families evacuated from the rocky Isle 110 miles from the Scottish mainland. Catherine was nine years and Rachel six when the final 42 inhabitants led by their grandmother, the Queen of St Kilda, decided to leave the Island. On the mainland they scattered to pursue their new lives. Catherine works as a cook in a hostel in Oban; a hostel for boys and lives in Lorne Avenue, Oban. Her sister, now Mrs Rachel Johnstone, lives in Shakespeare Avenue, Clydebank, Glasgow.
>
> Early in May 1979 the sisters planned a special cruise to St Kilda, but when they learned that they could not land they asked the army, which has a base there, to help them. The army came up with a plan to give the two sisters their once in a lifetime trip and yesterday the first stage of nostalgia was carried out. The sisters were picked up by army car at Dalmuir and driven to Rhu in Dumbarton, Glasgow. From there they sailed aboard the army's supply ship *Arakan* to the first stopover point, Loch Carnan, South Uist. Tomorrow on the early morning horizon the sisters will catch their first glimpse of St Kilda in 49 years. And at around 9 a.m. they will be put ashore to begin a six hour feast of nostalgia. Despite fond memories of their birthplace they have no delusions about their family's spartan existence in some of nature's most extreme conditions. 'It was a hard life indeed', said Catherine, 'Families lived by crofting, scraping a meagre living from the land; fishing was confined mainly to the better months and bird catching. I remember my father used to scramble down the cliffs – the

highest and steepest in Britain – to collect birds eggs for the table. Even after so many years I can picture it all in my mind.' On this special occasion they were met by the soldiers who man the radar that is located on Mullach Mhòr, and monitor test firings from the range on South Uist and members of the National Trust for Scotland, who are renovating houses in the village and rebuilding the Island school and church which was completed in August 1979.

In July 1966, I remember discussing St Kilda with Rachel who is a Mrs Johnson [*sic*]. She said, 'I had a dream about St Kilda. In my dream I saw No. 13, my home, and it looked just beautiful. Some day I hope that dream will come a reality', and on 7th July 1979, it did come true. Rachel went on to say, 'I don't remember life on the Island too clearly. Coming to the mainland seemed like another big adventure.' She continued to say that she could recall sleeping on the deck of the steamer on the trip to Argyllshire. It was a lovely crossing on a beautiful day. She continued to say that the mainland living has many advantages, but I have often wondered now what has been left behind. From the communication I received from Catherine and Rachel, they were delighted with their trip. The soldiers stationed on the Island went out of their way in order that the trip to the Island of their birth was as pleasant as it could be humanly possible. Donald and Christine, their parents, died a few years ago and are buried in Kiel cemetery, Lochaline, Argyllshire. Rachel, who was six years old leaving the Island, attended school in Larachbeg and married Ronald Johnson from Luss twenty-two years ago. They have two sons: 20-year-old Ronald and Malcolm 18 years. Ronald works as a draftsman in Clydebank Shipyard and Malcolm works in the post office.

Simplicity of Life on St Kilda

In reference to the law on the Island, what law was necessary among the inhabitants was administered by the resident missionary or minister acting with the Kirk session. Within living memory there had been no case meriting the attention of the civil authorities. The misdemeanors were small, generally someone miscalling someone else but the penalty of being denied communion for a certain length of time was one of which in a highly religious community every man and woman stood in dread. We had no music with which to entertain ourselves, not even a set of pipes. In my day on the Island the only musical instrument was a mouth organ and on a long winter evening we passed the time carding wool and talking about the happenings of the day.

How many birds I caught, how far did I go, did I reach Mullach Bi or Cambier during my visit to the Island in 1966? The cliffs had not changed, the Island houses derelict with the exception of a few that the National Trust of Scotland had renovated, and the wind and the birds have taken over. The Island was evacuated in 1930 and the inhabitants scattered between Lochaline in Argyllshire, the Black Isle, and Kincardine on Forth.

[*Our Trip Back to St Kilda in 1976*]

My uncle A. G. Ferguson visited St Kilda every year since 1903 but was unable to visit during the war years. When he was 77 years of age, in a 25 foot boat he made a trip to the Island. He was certainly a good sailor. The wife and I in 1976 visited Scotland for the sole purpose of visiting the Isle of my birth. I was anxious for the wife to see St Kilda so we boarded the *Uganda* in Glasgow on a Saturday evening and sailed round 8 p.m. heading for St Kilda on the National Trust of Scotland annual tour and arrived at St Kilda Sunday evening.

The first indication that we had that we were nearing St Kilda was the sound of the foghorn, surely the most mournful note to chill the heart of all passengers on board that were anxious to see St Kilda and the surrounding Islands. The north Atlantic was blanketed with thick white fog. I must say it was no consolation to hear from the ship's crew that they had never expected conditions like these in five years' experience of the St Kilda run. Back on the deck we peered through the fog, sometimes imagining we were seeing islands looming ahead. The captain over the loud-speaker said, 'You will never see anything looking out at eye level; you've got to look up there.' Dutifully we raised our eye level, and quite suddenly out of the whiteness planed a gannet, surely the most graceful of all sea birds, then there was another and another and suddenly the sky was full of them. I would say thousands of these silent birds were wheeling around us. I suppose we all saw the peak of the stac rising out of the fog at the same moment. It was Stac Lee, black and jagged towering out of the sea, and then we saw Stac An Armin and Boreray, the landscape of dreams on the sea. There were rafts of puffins, then the fog closed in again and we were left wondering if we had imagined the whole thing.

Naturally the wife and I and many others were greatly disappointed that we did not see the main Island, Hirta, the Village Bay. Some maintain there is no such place as St Kilda. The story goes that a careful mapmaker wrote on his chart not only the Gaelic word *tobar*, which means a well, but also its equivalent in old Norse, *childe*; what he wrote was in fact 'well, well'. As Scotland has a long tradition of dedicating wells to saints, it was thought that this well on the lonely Island of the Atlantic was dedicated to a saint called Childe or St Kilda. They tell me there is no such saint in any hagiography but the name stuck and is applied to the group of Islands consisting of Hirta, Boreray, Dun, Soay, Stac Levenish, Stac An Armin, Stac Birrock and Stac Lee. During my life on the Island to my mind I have never heard the name of the Island discussed. So, as far as I am concerned, the name is ideal regardless of what way it came into being.

[*Norman Gillies*]

Norman Gillies, a nephew of mine, at the age of 11 was one of the thirty-six inhabitants of the Island of Hirta who were evacuated by HMS *Harebell* on 29th August 1930. I visited him on several occasions at his own home in Chelmsford, England. He works in Ipswich running a paint and paper store. I discovered his memories of that day were a little hazy. I'm glad that the opportunity presented itself, that Norman was able to spend a fortnight on the Island with the working party of the National Trust of Scotland. I'm certain when I shall meet him again, God willing, that he would have a story to tell. He served with great distinction in His Majesty's Navy during the last Great War.

Norman's mother, who was my sister-in-law, who was taken from the Island in the beginning of 1930, Mary Gillies, was ill with acute appendicitis. On 30th January the captain of the fishing trawler *Caldew* contacted the GPO [General Post Office] in Edinburgh and told officials of the situation. It took two weeks before the various Government departments involved agreed to send help. On 15th February 1930 the fishery cruiser *Norna* sailed from Tarbert, Harris, to take Norman's mother Mary Gillies off the Island and deliver mail and food supplies to the community. The help was too late in coming; Mary was carefully taken aboard the *Norna* only to die in Stobhill Hospital, Glasgow, two days later. Norman was raised by his grandmother Annie Gillies, who was my mother. Norman went to school in Larachbeg, in the area of Lochaline.

In many ways the man of today is quite different from the man of a hundred years ago. His customs are different, his clothes are different, his surroundings are different but basically man's needs are always the same. He needs salvation, forgiveness for sin, guidance along life's pathway and a future hope that sustains him in the turmoil of the present day. In other words, he needs God and all that God in Christ and through the Holy Spirit can do for him.

[*Rev. Donald Ferguson and his Brother, Alex Ferguson*]

My uncle, the Rev. Donald Ferguson, was born in St Kilda, the third of a family of four of Donald Ferguson, who lived at No. 4 Main Street. He left the Island as a young man. Alex his brother was already established in Glasgow. On arriving in this city, he joined a shipyard in Partick, Glasgow, and became an apprentice in the carpenter trade.

He continued working in the same shipyard; as he was a conscientious worker he wasn't very long before he was promoted to foreman's job. During the First World War he was appointed as assistant superintendent. During the War all the shipyards throughout Great Britain were working three shifts a day, seven days a week. It is worthy of noting that this St Kildian refused to work on the Sabbath day, and those in authority respected this. He told me on one occasion the superintendent came to him and asked him would he work on a special work that had to be done on the Lord's day, and also this project was urgent. He agreed that he would on a certain condition: if he was allowed to work without pay. This was agreed upon. From his youth up he certainly adhered to the fourth commandment, 'Remember the Sabbath day to keep it holy.' He married a Uist lady from Grimsby, one who was attractive, intelligent, hospitable and a Christian lady. Their family consisted of four girls and two boys. The younger son died at the age of three, the younger daughter died a few years ago and also the oldest. Surviving: Mary, who is a nurse; Rachel, who is a widow; and the Rev. Donald Ferguson, who is pastor of the Free Church in Strathpeffer, Ross-shire.

I remember as a young lad my uncle visiting the Island of his birth; this is his first visit I remember. As we were walking past No. 9 Main Street on his way to his sister's home, No. 15 Main Street, he stopped and said 'Look at that million pound view of the water and the mountains.' He said, 'I to the hills will lift my eye from whence does come mine aid.' He left the ship building yard and studied at Edinburgh University and the Theological College of the Free Church.

My Visit to the Island of my Birth in the Summer of 1966

The change was amazing: roads built, cars and trucks running about, a massive helicopter landing base which is used on high days and holidays, abandoned oil drums and the noise of heavy Army transport, which to my mind would cause the early St Kildians to vibrate, if not turn, in their grave. The Island to me and many others will always belong to the early inhabitants and should be preserved at all costs. I'm sure the environment can be saved by careful corporate planning where the Island and the army can cohabitate with little lasting effect. I noticed electricity, fresh bread made daily and a club where alcoholic drinks were served, named Puffin's Club. This is something that was unknown to the Islander, movies etc., but this is a small comfort to the environmentalist, historian, or botanist who wants to observe the Island for what it was and is prepared to dispense with some of today's creature comforts which are so readily taken for granted.

As I stood at the very spot where we had a winch which we used to haul the boats, this winch was operated by human power. In its place today is a memorial cairn. Looking towards the army huts, the road built right up to Mullach Mhòr to the radar station, a journey that would take me barefooted an hour to arrive at mountain top. I was taken in a jeep to the radar spot on the mountain. I timed it in 12 minutes. The National Trust of Scotland to whom the Island belongs has with hard work and insufficient funds restored much of the early St Kildian way of life and hardships. I heartily agree with George Forbes' article on St Kilda, thinking there was little or no comparison between the lifestyle of the present occupants and that of the original Islanders. There is every comfort and luxury provided for the army including adequate transport, by sea and air if required. This I do not grudge; I experienced on the Island being for month and month with no communication with the outside world, the type of a life which meant loneliness. This I would not wish on anyone.

How does this compare with the hardships which were suffered by the original local inhabitants or as George Forbes prefers to describe the 'shaggy-haired rock climbing crofters, who for generations battled against the elements until they were finally obliged to accept evacuation to the mainland, the reasons being that they could not be guaranteed the necessary supplies being delivered by sea, owing to the severe gales in the winter which cut off the Islands'. It seems to me ridiculous when you look back today but it is typical of the thinking of the powers that be. If a fraction of the cost had been applied by Government it would have solved the problem and guaranteed that the Islanders could have continued to live contented in their rightful birthplace to this day, even alongside the army.

[*My First Visit to Lochaline in 1937*]

My first visit to Lochaline was the summer of 1937. The wife and I sailed from Sydney, Nova Scotia, in May 1937 on the SS *Nova Scotia*, a passenger ship which sailed from Boston calling at Halifax, Nova Scotia, but on account of 1937 being a coronation year, this ship made a special trip to Sydney and took aboard twenty-seven passengers. It sailed from Sydney to St John's Newfoundland and took aboard another twenty-one passengers and from there to Liverpool, England. Arriving in Lochaline the last week of May, we found my family contented with their new surrounding, glad that they were on the mainland where medical services were available to them when needed.

In conversation with my two brothers and my mother, I discovered that three people were outstanding in bringing the evacuation to a reality, namely my uncle Neil Ferguson, Mr Dugal Munro, missionary, and the resident nurse Barclay.

[*Neil Ferguson, St Kilda's Busiest Man*]

Men who are distinguished by the number and variety of their accomplishments should find out what Neil Ferguson has done for many years for the Islanders. A great many of the jobs he was responsible for, as mother indicated to me, he inherited from his father and his father's father holding the post before him. He was postmaster and postman, school manager who signed the register and personally conducted examinations. He was the elder of the Kirk, which entailed him to be responsible for all the church services during the missionary's absence. The missionary was entitled to a month's holiday on the mainland and often he took six weeks during his mainland visit. He had to see that he had sufficient supply for the long winter. He had also to see that the school was supplied with the necessary books for the various grades, ink and chalk; everything it took to run a school. So my uncle was in charge of the congregation of St Kilda during the missionary's absence, ground officer representing the estate of St Kilda, and its administration during my days on the Island. My grandfather was responsible for these jobs with the exception of running the post office. Neil was responsible for measuring out the fulmar oil and feathers tendered in kind for rent. Allotting the lamb pasturage on the Dun which is the proprietor's property.

Giving his consent to go to Soay for the purpose of taking sheep from Soay for the Islanders' use, two sheep as a general rule were allotted to each family for their consumption. When the navy men left the Island of St Kilda early 1919, Neil was also left with the responsibility of looking after the four point seven gun to see that it was greased and polished. Neil was offered a part-time job in the post office in Manish, Harris. It was also suggested to him that he could start up a store; however, having no experience along this line of running a store he declined the offer so he accepted a job with the Forestry Commission at Tulliallan. This he enjoyed for a number of years. He became greatly interested in the church, with the result he was made an elder in the Church of Scotland in Kincardine. By this congregation he was greatly respected. One Sunday morning as he was entering the church he took a heart attack and passed on to his eternal reward.

[*Dugald Munro*]

Mr Dugald Munro was the missionary who played a great part in the evacuation of the Island. He was the man that prepared the petition that the Islanders signed, supervised it and every person on the Island signed asking to be removed from the Island, to the mainland. Mr Munro was their spiritual adviser, schoolmaster and registrar. He was responsible to pack all the manse furniture, some of it going back almost to the days of the Apostle of the North, Dr MacDonald of Ferintosh. He had to pack the communion elements which consisted of the common cup, two silver plates for the bread and also to unscrew from the wooden walls of the little church the eight lamps of brass that lit the services during the winter nights. Not only that it lit the church in the winter but that was the only heat that was available: no stove. The school that was adjacent to the church had a fireplace and peat was used; each pupil took turns in taking a peat to school in order to keep the school fire burning. Also he had to pack all the books that were in the school library, so Mr Munro was an exceptionally busy man.

At last the *Harebell* arrived in Village Bay. Mr and Mrs Dugald Munro and their two children Donald and Megan boarded the *Harebell* in Village Bay. The moment they were aboard, the *Harebell* moved out of Village Bay and continued her voyage to Oban, arriving in Oban bay next evening at dusk. Those landed first were the Munros and their family, nurse Barclay and Dr Shearer. It goes without saying, out of mere curiosity crowds of holiday makers rushed to the pier to see the much advertised St Kildians, and reporters with cameras. This was something the St Kildians never heard of, and as my uncle said to me when I visited him in his own home at Tulliallan in the area of Kincardine, 'we were greatly annoyed by this publicity'.

However, whoever was in charge recognised this annoyance, placed the St Kildians in motor cars and rushed them to their hotels. Mr and Mrs Ferguson, postmaster and his wife were amongst those who were placed in a car and rushed to their hotel. This was the first experience of a hotel living. The Fergusons of course were met by an official of the Oban post office who took into custody the mail and documents and everything belonging to the post office in St Kilda. The missionary, Mr and Mrs Dugald Munro and family, went on a holiday to Easdale, his native place: a holiday well earned on account of his last couple of weeks on the Island were hectic, so many things to be looked after in the last day.

[*Matters Surrounding the Evacuation*]

The reason that prompted the evacuation, first I would say the British Government refusing to establish a regular mail service during all year round. I can recall on several occasions during my lifetime on the Island signing a petition and forwarding it to His Majesty's Government; the answer was no ship available to carry mail to the Island even once a month. The St Kildians had no one representing them in Parliament; they weren't given a chance to vote. I never saw a ballot box being distributed on the Island, if politicians took the trouble of coming to the Island looking for votes. In 1920 there were sixty people on the Island eligible for voting and if St Kilda had a voice in parliament I feel positive that life on the Island might have been a little easier. If there had been established a communication with the mainland on a regular basis, I know for a certainty that the Islanders would have been more contented, but as it was it was very unsatisfactory. Some winters we would be without mail for months and months at a time. The Islanders were grateful for the kindness of certain fishing trawlers that brought mail to St Kilda on their way to the fishing ground from Aberdeen, Grimsby, Hull and Fleetwood.

Another factor that caused the evacuation, during the First World War a Naval base was established on the Island and thirty men were housed in huts built east of the church. The relationship between these men and the Islanders was very friendly. I remember during the winter evenings one of these men visiting our home very regularly who could speak Gaelic. He hailed from the Island of Lewis in the Highlands of Scotland. Listening to him night after night describing the way of life on the mainland we youngsters came to the conclusion what an easy life they had in comparison to ours. We vowed, my younger brother and I, the moment we would arrive at a certain age that we too would leave the Island for a better and easier life on the mainland and this we did and the same was true of other youngsters our age, they also followed our example. This contributed to the evacuation of 1930.

The greatest blow to the Island was when the largest family on the Island in 1920 moved to the Isle of Lewis, namely William MacDonald No. 3 Main Street; eleven in the family. To see their home closed was a depressing sight and a great loss to the Island. William was the precentor in the Kirk and also acted as a janitor; church cleaned and lamps lit for the evening service and after the service responsible to see all lights out and everything belonging to the House of the Lord secured. He was a very religious man, as his older daughter Annie Bell who married one of the Naval men stationed on the Island, Kenneth MacLeod, a Lewis man, told me. She stayed behind with her father to see until everything was secured. When he put out the lights in the church his last chore was to kneel in prayer. The removal of this family from the Island which made life harder for those left behind, so this was another contributing factor to the evacuation of 1930.

St Kilda will remain as stern, rugged and lonely as ever. Huge waves in time of storm bouncing against the huge rocks. So the reason for such a flight of the inhabitants are already well known: reduced manpower in accessibility during autumn, winter and spring and the lack of medical assistance are some of the principal causes which bring in their train starvation, illness, and death. During my day on the Island I did experience starvation. The government in that instance came to our assistance, and also came to our aid during the flu epidemic; the time they converted the St Kilda church as a hospital and used the schoolhouse as a kitchen.

Life on the Island would have been more interesting if the Government had placed a registrar [*sic*] nurse on the Island continually. This they failed to do, they only did this occasionally. There was a very attractive home on the Island for the purpose of accommodating the nurse. The owners of the Island, MacLeods of Dunvegan, saw to this and the Islanders were very grateful to the MacLeods for this great service. Another factor that would have been a great help and satisfaction to the Islanders if there had been a resident wireless operator which meant communication with the outside world and especially in the case of sickness. My sister-in-law who died in Stobhill Hospital, Glasgow; her death took place on account of lack of communication. The Government was notified by a fishing trawler but it took the powers that be two weeks before they dispatched a Government vessel to the Island to take her to medical aid and when they did it was too late.

There was another death on the Island: a young girl who attended school and church with me. She took sick and in a month she passed away, the cause unknown. I remember that particular time that no fishing trawler or any kind of a vessel visited the Island so there was no way of communicating with the mainland.

One wonders what would have occurred if medical aid was available. This without a shadow of doubt influenced the Islanders to petition the Government to remove them from their Island home. As mother indicated unto me it was imminent, it had to take place; manpower that was left on the Island was now unable to carry on the necessary work to make a living. From mother and the rest of the Islanders that lived at Larachbeg told me that everyone on the Island was unanimous about this move. They all signed the petition, young and old to leave the Island. My mother told me that she sold one of her spinning wheels to one of the passengers on the SS *Dunra Castle* but she had one she never would part with and this was the last article she removed from No. 15 Main Street and she was still using it in her new home on the mainland at Larachbeg. Mother said to me I could not give up my life work so easily. From infancy I was taught to spin. In reference to the age of the spinning wheel that she kept as a precious possession, she said it would be well over 100 years. Her grandmother had it and this is far as she could go.

Let me report again from information gathered in 1937 from my people in Larachbeg in the area of Lochaline. The evacuation is the end of a movement that began with the war, that great instrument of social change. My brothers expressed the same opinion I shared all along. This is the way they put it: before the war the Island of Hirta was a recluse in his Island. Although it had no music, with the exception of the mouth organ, and no time to spare from the looms on the long winter night for the ceilidh, they were content for they knew no other life. But after the peace the young men went to the mainland and came back with news of other places, their romance and opportunities. The germ of knowledge of isolation was introduced and the loneliness followed. From August to March St Kilda is cut off from communication with the outer world, this caused the movement of the evacuation of 1930.

There were two ships that played a great role in the evacuation. On Wednesday 27th August 1930, *Dunra Castle* drops anchor in Village Bay. The mail for the last time comes ashore and is sorted out in St Kilda post office. The last letter I wrote from North River Victoria County, Cape Breton, Nova Scotia arrived in the last mail to St Kilda according to the information mother had. The sheep were loaded which took from morning to morning, started on Wednesday and finished loading at 1 a.m. on Thursday. At approximately 7 a.m. HMS *Harebell* enters into Village Bay. She has been sent by His Majesty's Government to carry out the evacuation of the Islanders and help them on their way to their new homes on the mainland.

Mother was telling me the last things she did. At 6 a.m. she paid her last visit to the cemetery; father and two brothers are buried in the Island cemetery. At 7 a.m. she locked the house and also the barn and pointing to the spinning wheel carried it with the family Bible to the jetty. She certainly paid a great compliment to the crew of the His Majesty's ship *Harebell.* They helped carry the last loads from the homes to the jetty. This help was apparently needed, especially assisting six widows. By 8 a.m., the last of the Islanders were embarked on the cruiser which raised anchor and steamed out of Loch Hirta, without a sound from the exiles. The cruiser left on her twelve hour voyage to Oban. All the Islanders I met in 1937 in Lochaline paid great compliments to the officers and crew of HMS *Harebell,* who were models of courtesy and consideration for their passengers during the trip, which was favoured with the same ideal weather conditions as attended the embarkation. They were notably attentive to the children of whom there were fourteen; three under school age. Tea and biscuits were constantly available and every wish of the passengers considered.

When the *Harebell* came abreast of Lochaline pier in the late afternoon, she was met by the *Princess Louise* from Oban, which had brought up the furniture and other effects of the St Kildians from the *Dunra Castle.* Eight of the ten families were disembarked. The reception on the shore of Morven was heart warming to the St Kildians as Mrs Donald MacDonald, our next door neighbour on the Island, and my mother stepped from the gang plank, both could not speak English to be met by a man who greeted them in the language they could understand: Gaelic. *'Tha mi toilichte gu bheil sibh an seo slan',* 'I'm glad to see you safely here'.

Transportation took them to their allotted place of abode. My mother, brother and nephew were not altogether happy with their place of abode in Ardness. Several things made them very dissatisfied: the smallness of the dwelling and its isolation from other homes, also their great concern that the school was a considerable distance away, and also the road in such a bad condition. Whoever was in charge of the arrangements did not take into consideration that the Islanders were living so close together within a stone throw of each other; this, I feel positive, contributed to discontentment. However it did not take long for those in authority to realise this and made the change to the betterment of all concerned.

When mother and the rest of the family were moved to Larachbeg, they were very thankful for the change and were very contented and happy. Here they were united once more with other natives as they were on the Island of Hirta. Thanks for His Majesty's Government for this adjustment. As I spent sixteen years of my ministry in the correctional field as a protestant chaplain in a federal penitentiary, I often thought of those who found themselves within the grey walls of the prison, the privileges they lost by being there. One thing they lost was their franchise, they could not vote in a provincial or federal election. I as a St Kildian living on the Island was treated in the same manner at an election time. No politician of any party made any attempt to gather votes on the Island. We were about forty miles from the nearest polling station if the Government of our time would have seen that we, the Islanders of St Kilda, were treated like other Highland Islands. Someone wrote at the time of the evacuation in one of the Scottish papers, with which I certainly heartily agree. The writer writes the following: 'we are about to leave an Island that has been inhabited since the second century. The subterranean house beside the nettle grown cemetery belongs to that epoch. The place names suppose a Celtic settlement. The Island is reputed to have been one time a penal settlement.' Many a day I thought along the same lines while I was working in the correctional field, that my birthplace was a prison, a sort of Devil's Island of the Hebrides to which inconvenient people were dispatched.

To its shores the notorious Lord Grange sent his wife to die for some Jacobite indiscretion. One of the few shafts of humour in its morbid history was the solemn declaration of Boswell to buy it so that he and his idol should winter there. As far as Lady Grange was concerned, yes she was a prisoner on the Island but she did not die there. According to the story, I heard from my people that she was transferred from the Island of St Kilda to Dunvegan in the Isle of Skye. St Kilda would have made an ideal penal prison. It could be another Alcatraz USA.

In many parts of the world today there are men and women whose hearts are moved, souls stirred by the oft recurring memories of their early experiences in St Kilda church. I remember many of the dear old souls who gathered there to worship God. They would listen, as I had to also, to the longest sermon. They were pilgrims on the way to another land, a land whose fruits were sweet to their taste. Long ago it was written that glorious things are spoken of the city of God. Without fear of contradiction, we say that this prophecy found its fulfilment in the St Kilda church. How true the words of the poet who sang: 'Then on memory's pages I can see again the church by the side of the road and where ever I roam, it is guiding me home.'

The church by the side of the road ringing the St Kilda church bell for the last time was the precentor who took over when

William MacDonald emigrated to the Island of Lewis. So Norman MacKinnon who resided in No. 1 Main Street, St Kilda became the church custodian and presenter. Norman had a large family; there were two sons, both over six feet.

Mr MacKinnon landing at Lochaline pier carried a hand lamp. He and Mrs MacKinnon evinced a great interest in their surroundings. Also with them eight daughters who were allotted a home in Larachbeg. They had a good voyage they said but Mrs MacKinnon added that the children had been sick and was very glad to find their feet on the mainland. Mr and Mrs MacKinnon had experience of the mainland but this was the sons' first time off the Island. In my conversation with the MacKinnons in 1937, they spoke warmly of the kindness that had been shown them by all on the *Harebell* during the voyage from St Kilda to Lochaline. Accompanying them was Finlay Gillies, the oldest man of the party. He is the father of Mrs MacKinnon. The number of people on the quay impressed some of the Islanders. Mrs MacKinnon told me that she was very curious about the large number of people on the pier and asked did they usually have this number when a ship arrives at the Lochaline pier. Apparently she did not get an answer to her question so she said the voyagers were soon conducted to their new home and the crowd dispersed.

While at Oban great crowds testified to the interest which the evacuation had aroused where Islanders were placed. Apparently the families were transported in relays as follows: Larachbeg – the MacKinnon family of ten including three foresters; Lochaline – widow MacQueen and widow Gillies and her two daughters; Ardness – John Gillies and mother and Norman John; Achabeg – Donald Gillies, his wife, two daughters Catherine and Rachel, this is my two brothers and mother; Savery – Mrs Kathrine Gillies and her two sons, Donald and Ewen, also Lachlin MacDonald, her brother. A large quantity of baggage was disembarked at Lochaline pier, which included the inevitable spinning wheels, various antique looking chairs, and other household furniture. The Island has not been completely denuded of furnishing. I was told on good authority that No. 11 Main Street, St Kilda, the newest house on the Island, that quite considerable furnishings were left in it.

The last Sabbath on the Island was indeed a memorial one. It was obvious to all that the church on the Island of St Kilda had finished its task. Nobly and well it served its days and generation, but now its labours were over. The St Kildians that were allotted to Lochaline were a great strength to the congregation of Kiel and also the congregation of Lochaline. They took an active part in all the organisations of the church. My brother was representative elder from Lochaline and Kiel church for many years; he enjoyed his fellowship with his brother elders. I recall him telling me about Lochaline and Kiel congregation and a visitation they made during the last two weeks of November when a team of elders supported by a few volunteers from the congregation visited every home except those where people were already members in Kiel on Lochaline. He said there was not one of the team who did not find the experience both interesting and rewarding. Almost without exception we were received in a most friendly way and this included people not of our own denomination. He continued to say a card with relevant information was completed for each household. They will be studied and followed up. Here was a St Kildian that fitted into the method and the way of the other elders that were raised in the neighbourhood. Talking with one of the elders in the community, Malcolm Gillies, he said, 'Your brother Donald is one of the finest elders in the parish, one that is well liked by all the members and adherents of the parish'. I was delighted to hear this compliment, not only he went on to say, all St Kildians became a tower of strength to our small congregation.

Rev. MacSween a Gaelic pastor and a Lewis man revealed to me in 1937 that the St Kildians got on well with all members and adherents of the congregation; they got on well with the natives of the mainland. St Kilda's abandoned eight families were disembarked at Lochaline pier in Morven where forestry work on the Ardtornish estate awaited them; they were guaranteed this before they left the Island. The remainder of the St Kildians continued on to Oban. Thus completed the evacuation of the Rocky Island that with its companions Soay and Boreray, stands as a lonely and storm-smitten sentinel in the remotest west. The operation was desired by the St Kildians for economic reasons and from every point of view was wise. Nevertheless it has not been without its almost epical moments of emotion.

A portion of the earth, howsoever forbidding it be, is not abandoned by all its inhabitants on one day without a deep stirring of the heart and the imagination. We can respond sympathetically to the genuine emotions which filled the hearts of the St Kildians as they gazed from the deck of the *Harebell* at the cone of Connacher and the jagged peak of Boreray receding and finally vanishing under the horizon. There was regret that the wild crags will test the strength of the egg gatherers no more, that the tiny fields will be forever untilled, that the bell of the church will call no worshippers to church on Sundays, that the St Kildian boats will put out for Boreray no more and smoke has vanished from the hearths in the straggling village. The Island has been left to the fulmars, gugas and gannets and its surrounding waters to the seals. A heritage of Pelagian existence has been broken after enduring for a thousand years and St Kilda enters into the company of desert Islands.

The regrets aroused throughout Scotland by the evacuation are natural enough but there is no excuse for the sort of sentiment that prompts people to argue that the Island is as fit a place for human habitation as ever it was; such a suggestion is without foundation in reality. For the past eighty years and more, the primitive economic life of the St Kildians has been in process of decay, and sooner or later the *Harebell* or a successor would have had to perform its affecting task. The irregular visits of trawlers and steamers brought the call of the mainland and the wider world to the youth of the wild Isle and the response has been such that during the past few years the manpower has been so depleted as to prevent necessary work from being undertaken. Contact with modern civilisation also accustomed the natives to a rather higher standard of living than was known to their bird-catching and pastoral forebears and lately they had come to be in some measure dependent on state aid. Their primitive Gaelic mode of living in fact had come to an end and the issue was one of life in new, hopeful and honorable circumstances or of a decrepit and anachronistic existence, unlit by any gleam of hope. The rejuvenation of St Kilda's economic resources was well nigh beyond human powers, and the elementary type of existence alone possible on her meagre meadow land served no purpose, either cultural, economic or genetic in the corporate life of the state. Evacuation was the only possible course open to the Islanders and the authorities.

To harbour regrets, therefore, would be to blind one's eyes to the facts. The St Kildian village community has now passed out of existence, and its surviving representatives have been launched upon a new life in new surroundings with every good wish and much practical help at their disposal. If there were any lasting regret needed, it would be that no literary artist of a generation or two past saw fit to do for St Kilda what J. M. Synge did for the Aran Islands, off the west coast of Ireland. That however would have no real bearing upon the present issue. The Islanders are taking up life on the mainland in circumstances that are both favourable and hopeful. The afforestation areas present their inhabitants with opportunities for combined sylvan and agricultural work, with occasional fishing added and a healthy life and reasonable livelihood is possible for all willing men. The St Kildians are, we believe, capable of adjusting themselves to the tasks before them. Since many of them have at one time or another paid brief visits to the Outer Isles or the mainland, the broader aspects of modern life will be already familiar to them. Those who perchance have never seen a horse or tree before will not be desolated and unnerved by the new experience. The transplanting of the Island community is of course somewhat in the nature of adventure, but it is an enterprise that should have no harmful or disastrous issue. The children of these new settlers will have the whole highlands and beyond before them when their time comes to take up a station in life. The growing heritage of the new era of forestry and hydro electric power will be theirs.

[*My Visit to Scotland in 1967*]

During my visit to Scotland in 1967, I visited the Island of Lewis. I spent 48 hours on the Island. These hours were spent with a second cousin of mine, a widow who lived on a small croft in Lenishader in the area of Callanish, Lewis. Annie Belle was married to a very fine Christian man by the name of Kenneth MacLeod. Annie Belle met her husband on the Island of St Kilda as Kenneth was one of the Naval men stationed on the Island during the First World War. Kenneth was a Gaelic speaker and was able to talk with those on the Island that were unable to speak English. He was greatly thought of by all the Islanders. They were married in Stornoway after the First World War. Annie and I went to school together. During my visit to her home, the conversation was about the days we spent on the Island of Hirta. She reminded me that they as a family were the first to leave the Island. She continued to say, 'We all lived as one big family and this was the first final break in the community, I'm sure they felt just the same as we were feeling departing from them; but it was a beginning of a new life for us'.

I visited in 1967 a Norman MacKinnion who lived in The Black Isle. He was the oldest son of Norman who lived at No. 1 Main Street and who was the precentor of the St Kilda parish who rang the church bell for the last time and also precented the last psalm at the last service that was held in the St Kilda church. The psalm was number 72 and the last three verses; 17 to the end, 'His name shall endure forever. His name shall be continued as long as the sun, and men shall be blessed in him! All nations shall call Him blessed.' I asked Norman Junior, 'Are you happy with the evacuation of 1930?' His answer came readily, 'I have no regrets', he said. 'Right enough it was sad leaving the Island but however, no matter how sad it may have seemed at the time, it was beneficial'.

When I left St Kilda in 1924

In 1924 I left my native Island on the SS *Hebrides* bound for the largest city in Scotland, Glasgow. I left St Kilda on Thursday and arrived in Glasgow on Monday afternoon. It was a shock. I was totally amazed to see metal things running about on four wheels. I was met by a first cousin of mine, the late Donald Ferguson who left St Kilda in 1924. I had two uncles in Glasgow, Alexander and Donald. So I stayed for approximately a week with my uncle and aunt who had a very attractive home in Old Kilpatrick. I left every morning with my uncle to his office at 93 Hope Street, Glasgow. He was a sales man for St Kilda and Harris Tweed. During that week I used to deliver patterns to various shops in Glasgow which presented me with the opportunity of finding my way in this large city and also to get familiar with city life.

I was employed by the Clyde Trust Company and I was assigned to a dredger which was dredging opposite the city of Greenock. I remained with this company for a year. At the end of the year I left and entered the Bible Christian Institute on Bothwell Street, Glasgow, aiming at becoming a missionary at home or abroad. After spending a session in this institution I decided to leave and study to become a clergyman. With this in my mind I registered in Skerry's College preparing myself for further studies in Glasgow University. I was appointed by the Free Church of Scotland to a mission hall on the south side of the city. The hall was on Eaglesham Street and services were held every Sunday night at a salary of one pound a week. This was in the year 1926.

My first attempt to visit the Island was in 1937. I left Oban on one of MacBrayne boats and landed in Lochmaddy. On Saturday morning I visited a next door neighbour of mine that I had on the Island. I lived at No. 15 Main Street and he lived at No. 16 Main Street. He was a resident missionary at Lochportan in Uist. I spent a very enjoyable weekend with him and his wife and preached for him twice on Sunday at 11 a.m. and also at 6 p.m.; the two services were in Gaelic. Naturally our conversation was based on the evacuation of the Island. Donald's remark was it should have taken place years before it took place. He maintained making a living on the Island was a hard one, hard work and getting nowhere. He went on to say that he had no regrets leaving the Island. He reached standard six in school; so far as the education on the Island was concerned, that's as far as one could go. Donald was attracted to leave the Island and seek work in Harris. Lord Leverhulme commenced to build a large fish plant in Harris and this project was to employ a large number of people. Apparently this was only a rumour, a plant that never was even started.

So Donald made his way to Glasgow and found work in a ship building yard in Clydebank working during the day but attended evening classes at the Bible Training Institution on Bothwell Street, Glasgow. He graduated in 1932. The United Free Church of Scotland appointed him to his first mission charge in Islay. From there to Lochportan in Uist, from Lochportan to Scalpay, Harris, and from Scalpay, Harris, to Callanish in Lewis, which was his last charge. He retired in the early 1970s to Obbe, Harris. His wife was a native of Obbe and they had one son who is in business for himself on the mainland outside Oban.

Donald in his chosen profession was well liked by all the congregations he served. He was the only St Kildian that served in this capacity. He passed on a few years ago to his eternal reward. It could be truly said of him, well done good and faithful servant, thou wert faithful in few things, enter into the joy of thy Lord. On Monday morning I travelled to Lochmaddy and waited till 4 p.m. to board the SS *Hebrides* that was on its way to St Kilda; however, I was disappointed in this trip. The captain spoke to me and revealed to me the sad news on account of the wind being from the southeast that there was no hope of landing on St Kilda and, instead of going to St Kilda, he landed at Tarbert, Harris. So I left the ship and took a bus to Stornoway and visited with widow Mrs William MacDonald who was the first family to leave the Island. Her husband passed away in 1936. He was the Island precentor.

She was living with her two youngest daughters in a home in Stornoway.

I asked her what she thought of the evacuation of the Island. She said that she was extremely sad when the news of the evacuation came to her. She thought of the happy time that she had on the Island during her sojourn; the community spirit was just excellent, 'Nevertheless my husband and I found it very hard to raise eleven of a family, the Naval men visiting our home continually describing life on the mainland and our oldest boy in the army; and when he was home on his last leave he urged us to leave the Island, and to give the rest of the family a chance to better themselves on the mainland. This and the pressure from our family prompted us to leave, which indeed was for our betterment.' Mrs MacDonald revealed to me the hardship and also the worry that confronted them on several occasions: 'just think of shoes that had to be provided for eleven; and also to keep enough food on the table at times was not an easy job.

'The last February on the Island was an extremely hard one, not only for us but for all the Islanders. The year I believe was 1921, there were seventy-five inhabitants on the Island and all were in fairly good health but some families were completely out of flour and sugar and some were out of potatoes. The potatoes that they had set aside for seed had to be used. Those who had supplies shared them as far as they would go among their neighbours,' she said. 'My husband and I prayed earnestly that relief would come in our direction and Donald', she said, 'God answered our prayer. Here after our plight the day and night before, here a Fleetwood trawler arrived in Village Bay and here we were saved once again from starvation', and she said in addition to that, 'The arrival in Village Bay of the ship *Sarpendon* of the Blue Funnel Line, the directors of the shipping company on a maiden voyage in their new passenger liner, having been generous enough to land sufficient stores of food to keep all the Islanders alive until the *Hebrides* arrived in late May. So, experiencing this, my husband and I decided to leave the Island and gave our family a chance to educate themselves and find an easier way of making a living. And I can say that our prayer was answered and all of them found employment, others of them got married, the two oldest girls, and all are very happy with their lot in life.

'The Lord has been', said she, 'certainly good to us'. Placing in my hand the Gaelic family Bible they took from the Island of St Kilda, and I read psalm 46, 'God is my refuge and strength' and both of us kneeled in prayer. She was certainly an outstanding Christian. Her last words were in Gaelic, 'I do know that my Redeemer liveth.' I certainly enjoyed that afternoon with her; I received great strength and courage from this Godly woman's faith. In the living room where we were, it was to me as if it was to God's servant of old when he said 'this is none other but the House of God and the very gate of Heaven'.

[*Larachbeg in 1937*]

During my sojourn in Larachbeg on my first visit to my family in 1937, one Sunday afternoon in my mother's home a company of St Kildians gathered: there was Lachlan MacDonald, who has his home at Ben Nevis, Mrs Norman MacKinnon, Donald my brother and John, widow Gillies from Savery and Norman MacKinnon Junior. Each spoke of their experience since coming to the mainland, comparing life on the Island as they expressed their joys, sorrows, success and disappointments. Nevertheless none of them regretted leaving the Island. The only regret expressed by one and all was that they felt that they did not thank those who arranged the move from the Island to the mainland. Lachlan expressed it in a very magnificent way, he went on to say, 'Why are we so grudging with our praise, so tongue tied when it comes to saying thank you? The love and cherishing that encompassed us at home in St Kilda and also here on the mainland of Morven, the visits that we are enjoying with our new friends, the beauty and the peace of our present surroundings – all these and so much more we take for granted. Instead our hearts should be so full that praise and thanks well up like water from a fountain, spontaneous and unconfined'.

He said, 'Years ago I heard a story of an old Scottish divine who modified his grace before meat according to what was set before him. From time to time, when visiting outlying parts of his parish, we would be invited to share the midday meal with some of his flock. If the food was salt herring, a dish he heartily disliked, he would say, "For the least of these thy mercies", but if the farmer had recently killed a lamb and if there was a roast of lamb for dinner, he was moved to a more fervent thanksgiving, "Bountiful Creator, for thy great gifts of course there should be neither limit nor condition in our thanksgiving." '

Lachie recalled the words of a hymn he heard in the Kiel Parish Church, Morven on a thanksgiving Sunday, his first thanksgiving on the mainland. The words of the last verse went something like this, 'What should be in our hearts we could well echo a prayer of George Herbert when he asks, O God you have given so much to us, give us one thing more – a thankful heart'. And the gathering that evening in that home agreed whole heartily with Lachlan's version of thanksgiving.

I was asked to conduct worship and I can recall asking mother what was the last portion you read in the old home on St Kilda. She readily answered, handing me the Bible she used last in St Kilda and read the forty-sixth psalm, 'God is our refuge and strength, a very present help in trouble' and finished the devotion with prayer and benediction, 'The blessing of God Almighty, the father the son and the holy spirit be with you all now and ever more'. All enjoyed a cup of tea afterwards and evening well spent. A few children were there, also Rachel Gillies, Rachel MacKinnon and Norman Gillies.

During my visit in 1937 I also visited the following; all of them left St Kilda before the evacuation of 1930. My first call was on the south side of Glasgow, here I visited John MacQueen, son of Finlay MacQueen who lived at No. 2 Main Street, St Kilda. Finlay, the famous cragsman on the Island of St Kilda, John was employed as a watchman on Mullach Mhòr during the First World War. John left the Island of St Kilda at the end of the first war. He worked for the Clyde Trust Company. Before he retired he was first mate on one of the barges that sailed daily to the Tail of the Bank. He married a very attractive lady from Point in Lewis at Ross-shire, Scotland. His brother Norman became a deep sea sailor. He sailed all over the world. He visited me here in Vancouver. He was married to a Tiree girl and had a very lovely home in Partick, Glasgow. Angus MacDonald worked in a shipyard in Clydebank and was elevated to a foreman and married an Old Kilpatrick girl and had one son that emigrated to New Zealand and is in business for himself in Auckland. The wife and I visited him in 1974. All these St Kildians did exceptionally well in their chosen profession.

My brother Neil married a Glasgow lady and they had a very attractive home in Garthamlock in Glasgow, Scotland. He too enjoyed his shipyard work, watchman on the Broomielaw Dock, and also as a watchman on the Island of his birth, St Kilda. So all these Islanders were well thought of by those who employed them.

[*My Time Staying in Govan Cross, Glasgow*]

I remember being in lodgings near Govan Cross, Glasgow. My landlady was a Lewis woman and she was a member of the Govan Free Church, which was approximately four blocks from her home. The minister of the Govan Free Church was Rev. A Fraser, a native of Inverness whom I knew exceptionally well. I was a member of Hope Street Free Church, my minister was Rev. John MacLeod, OBE; a church I attended regularly every Sunday. The landlady drew to my attention that they were having a guest speaker from Canada preaching in the Govan Free Church the first Sunday in March 1926 so I decided that I would attend the Govan Free Church on this special Sunday: Rev. A Mackay, minister of St James Church, London, Ontario, Canada, a native of Inverness, Scotland. He spoke on the text John 3 and 16, 'For God so loved the world that he gave his only begotten son, whosoever believeth in Him should not perish, but have everlasting life.' I enjoyed his sermon immensely.

When he finished the sermon he closed the Bible and addressed the congregation. He related his mission to Scotland and Ireland. He told the story of the union that had taken place in Canada between the Congregational Methodist and Presbyterian churches in Canada. He said, 'I'm a continuing Presbyterian.' The continuing Presbyterian Church had 800 congregations, 300 of those congregations are without a settled clergyman. He said, 'If there is any one present in this audience that would like to discuss with me the possibilities that the Presbyterian Church in Canada is offering to young men studying for the ministry, I would love to meet with such at the close of the service.' So I grasped the opportunity and had a very profitable session with him outside the door of the church. He set a date that he would visit me at my lodging place.

He, being a Gaelic speaker, understood perfectly the need of Gaelic speakers in Glengarry County in Ontario, Gaelic congregations in the eastern townships of Quebec and the great number of Gaelic congregations in various parts of Cape Breton in Cape Breton County, Victoria County and Inverness-shire County. On his visit to my abode, a visit where he described the advantages of continuing my studies in Canada. The salary of a student missionary on the mission field during the summer month was £10 a Sunday, board and room provided by the congregation. Here I discovered that there was no comparison to the wages I was receiving from the Free Church: £1 a week and provide your room and board out of that. As my St Kildian parents were unable to help me financially and as I was determined to go through for the Christian ministry, I assured the Rev. MacKay if my application was acceptable that I was in readiness to proceed to Canada and would accept a mission church anywhere in the Dominion of Canada.

I received a letter from the headquarters of the church in Toronto appointing me to a congregation in Cape Breton, the parish of North River and North Shore in Victoria County. The problem that faced me now was how I was to secure the money that would pay for my passage on the SS *Metagama*. Looking into my purse I could only find in it six shillings and six pence. This was my whole fortune. I asked the Lord for guidance for my devotion that night, I said, 'Lord if it be thy will direct me to a portion of Scripture that would encourage me to undertake this journey to an unknown land'. In my room in Govan that night as I took up the Bible in my hand, here it opened at the book of Exodus chapter 3, the story of Moses when he received the call from God at the burning bush that he was to be the leader that was capable of leading the children of Israel out of Egypt into the Land of Promise. I received great comfort from verse 12, 'And he said, certainly I will be with thee: and this shall be a token unto thee that I have sent thee: when thou hast brought forth the people out of Egypt, ye shall serve God upon this mountain.'

The next day I was to sit an exam for a bursary of a £100 in the living room of my minister's house that was in the Kelvinside district of the city of Glasgow. If I was successful, this would be a great help to me to pay my fare from Glasgow to Quebec City in Canada.

Two weeks after I wrote this exam I received in the mail £100. Immediately I paid my fare of £50, got a passport and other few things that I needed and landed aboard the boat with one pound in my pocket. Sailed from Glasgow at the end of April and landed in Quebec City on 7th May, which was a Sunday, with one sixpence in my pocket but I had a letter in my possession stating that transportation would be paid from the port of landing to the congregation I was appointed to. I looked for a Presbyterian Minister at the landing pier but I was unable to locate one. However I met an Anglican clergyman that directed me to the Presbyterian manse in the city of Quebec. This Samaritan phoned the Rev. Gordon, a bachelor who received me with open arms, had lunch with him and immediately after lunch he and I proceeded to the immigration shed. He got my luggage, bought a ticket for me to Sydney, Cape Breton, Nova Scotia and also he gave me twenty dollars.

By the time I arrived at my destination at North River, Victoria County, Cape Breton, I had only 50 cents to my name. I found myself in the home of Dan A. MacLeod, one of St Andrews church elders, arriving on Saturday evening. Next Sunday I had to preach twice, once in Gaelic and the other in English. Attendance at each service was well over two hundred. I was informed that there was death in the congregation and that I had to conduct the funeral at 2 p.m. on Monday from the house. Arrangements were made for transportation, so on Monday 9th May 1927 [*sic*] the son arrived at the house where I was boarding. So here I got my first ride in with a horse and buckie [*sic*]. The night before I went over the service with my host Dan A. MacLeod, this was the first funeral I conducted. Arriving at the home I found it crowded, as I entered into the living room the first thing I saw was a man in the casket all dressed up. He was wearing one of the old fashion collars with a bow tie. I was stunned; I never expected to see a corpse dressed up in that fashion. After I got over the first shock I took the second look. Now in being honest, the first thought that came to my mind was this, the old man dressed and nowhere to go. I was looking for what I was accustomed to on the Island of St Kilda, all bodies were dressed in a shroud and naturally this was what I expected. However I got soon accustomed to it because this is the Canadian custom.

[*My Various Posts*]

My first summer on the mission field of the Presbyterian Church in Canada was indeed a very enjoyable one. People were kind, hospitable and sympathetic. With my summer remuneration, and the generous gift from the congregation I was able to commence my studies in McGill University in Montreal. The Cape Bretoners hailed from Lewis, Harris, Skye, Lochinver and Uist. To substantiate this, one finds Highland names in the Highlands of Nova Scotia such as Skye, Glen Tarbert, Ben Nevis, Tolsta, Dell and Stornoway. These names indicate that people from the above mentioned places came from there and named their new land, names that they were accustomed in the Highlands of Scotland. I served this congregation two summers: 1927 and 1928. I spent the summer of 1929 in Dunvegan Ontario, the summer of 1930 Marsboro, Quebec, 1931 and 1932 Milan Quebec and graduated in 1933. I served a mission field in Killarney Manitoba, was ordained in Knox church, Carberry Manitoba July 1932, serving Carberry for a year. In September 1935, I received a call from the parish of North River and North Shore.

It is worthy of noting that St Andrews North River Church was the first pulpit I stood in, in Canada. What a coincidence that I would be inducted after graduation from the Presbyterian College, Montreal. I served this congregation until September 1938 when I received a call from Mira Ferry and Catalone and was inducted into this pastoral charge October 1939. In April 1942 I resigned from the parish of Mira Ferry and Catalone and joined the army as a Canadian chaplain. I served with Pictou Highlanders in St Johns Newfoundland, Gender and Botwood and early 1943 returned to Halifax Nova Scotia.

I left Halifax early in 1944 and was stationed in England for a very short period of time. I went across the Channel in 1944 and became Padre of the 27th Canadian armoured regiment. I saw action in Belgium, Holland and Germany and I was at Williams Haven in Germany at the armistice and I met three St Kildians, two of them in the army and my nephew served in the Royal Navy. During the Second World War, St Kilda was inhabited and the Government made St Kilda a prohibited area.

I spent one New Year's Day with my uncle Alexander Ferguson and we spent the day in Dumbarton visiting his boat, the *Colonsay*. If the Government would have allowed him he would have visited St Kilda during the Second World War. He got a great joy and satisfaction during the war years visiting other Islands in the Highlands of Scotland and especially Harris. He used to climb up the highest hill in Leverburgh and on a clear day he said to me, pointing to binoculars in the boat, I could see Connacher, Oiseval and Boreray; Even from seeing the Island of his birth he got a great joy and satisfaction. I visited my mother four times during my sojourn in the country during the war.

Presbyterian Church Record: Chaplaincy Service, Church Group Overseas

The following appeared in the Record mentioned:

> a recent letter from Capt. D. J. Gillies, Canadian Army overseas, conveyed to us the above picture. In this connection it may be noted that Capt. Gillies has four services every Sunday. This is taken at the door of the chapel after a Sunday evening, voluntary service. The men are from all over Canada. A prayer meeting on Tuesday night has an attendance averaging 25 and the young people's society on Friday has an average of 20 in attendance. A Bible class is held on Tuesday evening before the regular prayer meeting with an average of 18 attending. Capt. Gillies says he has half a dozen good earnest workers, who are a very substantial help.
>
> Sunday school with their co-operation has been established with eight children, six to twelve years, attending for the first time. A recent Sunday night service brought together a company of over two hundred. Those under Capt. Gillies's care maintain interest in the general work of the church, as indicated by his forwarding a contribution of five dollars from an officer who is a member of Westminster church, New Glasgow, Nova Scotia, of which Dr Hugh Munro is minister. The officer commanding in his area is one of the best supporters of Rev. S. T. Macarthur in our church at Stellarton, Nova Scotia. Interest is shown also in the Presbyterian Record, for Capt. Gillies requests further copies be sent to him and to the chaplain of another unit. He concluded the letter with the following: 'the Gospel is good news, the gladdest news that ever broke upon the ear of man'. The four St Kildians that served in the Second World War were honorably discharged at the close of hostility.

I returned to Canada in February 1946 and landed in Winnipeg on a bitterly cold day, snow piled high everywhere you looked. I was given a month's leave so the wife and I decided to visit Vancouver, British Columbia, left Carberry Manitoba in middle

February, piles of snow everywhere you looked. We took the CP Rail to Vancouver and on arriving in that city, a beautiful day and no snow to be seen anywhere but the green grass. So after spending a couple of weeks in beautiful British Columbia we decided if the opportunity presented itself that we would just love to spend the remainder of our days at the coast. The congregation known as the Vancouver Heights presented a call to me. This I accepted and was inducted to the pastoral charge of Vancouver Heights Church in April 1946 and I received my discharge at Jericho Beach, Vancouver at the end of April 1946.

I served the Vancouver church from 1946 to October first 1952. I accepted the protestant chaplaincy in New Westminister Federal Penitentiary and served in this capacity from 1946 to 1966.

[*The National Trust Cruise to St Kilda in 1967*]

In 1967 I visited the old country Scotland and enjoyed the National Trust cruise to St Kilda. On arriving at St Kilda in the morning, a beautiful day, the sea calm, we stopped in Village Bay. Approximately an hour later I found myself on the bridge with the captain and members of the National Trust. I was asked to give a commentary of the history of the Island and as I looked to the west to the Island of the Dun I was reminded immediately of 1913: Angus Gillies who lived at No. 6 Main Street and my grandfather Donald Ferguson coming to school in a very excitable manner and asked the teacher to let them have the older boys in the school to launch a small boat. As a tragedy occurred at the Dun I was amongst those who launched that boat. Three men drowned, namely Norman MacQueen and his brother John. Norman lived at No. 11 Main Street, his brother John lived at No. 10 Main Street. The third person was Donald MacDonald who lived at No. 16 Main Street. Saved was my father John Gillies and Neil MacKinnon who lived at No. 1 Main Street. Beautiful day, sea calm but to my interpretation the small boat they used was overloaded. It was a canoe and these Islanders were not used to that type of a boat.

Then as I looked east, I was reminded of the schoolboy that was drowned fishing. This accident happened on Oiseval: two brothers and a neighbour were with him but none of them could swim. As I looked at Village Bay I was reminded of the day that I used to see in Village Bay whales anchored half a dozen at a time. At times when the wind was from the southeast the odour was not a pleasant one by any means.

The whales anchored also reminded me when a first cousin of mine, Neil Ferguson who visited the anchored whales and landed on one of them and fished sitting on the back of the whale for a couple of hours. There was a whaling station at Bunavoneadar in Harris, and these whales were towed to that station. The three whaling ships were from Norway. Looking towards the beach I was reminded of seeing the first vessel beached on the sand during the First World War in 1916 with a big hole in her bow on account of enemy action. Looking at Mullach Mhòr I was reminded of the many days I descended down that mountain with a big bag of peats on my back or coming down Oiseval with forty fulmars on my back. As I looked at the beach just below the croft of No. 9 Main Street I was reminded of half a dozen Islanders on the beach one afternoon in 1917. They discovered a big cask of rum. My uncle Neil Ferguson made this discovery but the contents of this cask was shared amongst the Islanders, each one receiving an equal share.

My last look was towards the spot where St Kilda Parliament used to meet, between No. 5 and No. 6. Here important decisions were made; should we commence to cut the peats or should we gather the sheep for shearing or should we build that barn for one of the widows on the Island that needed it; business of this nature that continually came before the gathering for discussion.

The boat then sailed the back of the Dun. First thing I brought to the attention of the tourists was when we came in sight of the Lover Stone. Passing this historic spot we came to Soay and I told them the story of Duncan who was placed there for destroying the first inhabitants of the Island by fire. He built himself an underground abode and it is still called Duncan's cave. We saw droves of

Soay sheep on the move which reminded me of the days that I also visited Soay with other Islanders to catch sheep for our own consumption. As we came around to the north, in front of us was North Bay. I tried to describe to the tourists the spot that great Highlander evangelist Dr John MacDonald of Ferintosh landed. He was unable to land in Village Bay on account of bad weather. I also endeavoured to show the tourists the well he had his first drink on St Kilda and the St Kildians built a *cleit* over that well which is still in good shape. Dr MacDonald changed the life of the Island; brought to them the pure Gospel, built the church and saw to it that education was established on the Island. The Islanders thought the world of him. His name was a household name; no one could take Dr MacDonald's place.

I showed the tourists at the back of Connacher where two men lost their lives on the first day harvesting fulmars, the only accident that occurred on the Island during my sojourn there. We headed for Stac an Armin, Stac Lee and Boreray. Sheep could be seen on Boreray and I tried to show the tourists the location of the three underground abodes used by the Islanders during their week on Boreray shearing the sheep. I also told the story of the death that took place there. One could not see the sky at times for gannets flying above the ship and the sea covered with puffins – quite a sight. Enjoyed this tour immensely.

[*My Visit to Neil and Mary Ann Ferguson*]

On arriving back in Glasgow, the next day I visited with my first cousin Neil Ferguson and his wife Mary Ann at Kincardine and had tea with them. The conversation at the tea table was my experience on the National Trust cruise, especially the hour spent in Village Bay, St Kilda. Entering the Bay to me was like entering a ghost town. Looking at No. 1 Main to No. 16 Main, no movement of any kind in comparison to the days he and I lived there, dogs barking, people watching the steamer entering Village Bay, and every able-bodied man making for the jetty, everyone excited, boats launched and rowed out to the vessel in Village Bay. Life as it should be, this was the custom in our day. The Island looked dead to me, it made me very sad looking at the mountains you and I used to travel looking for sheep or cutting peats on those mountains, or building a *cleit*, always something to do.

Neil reminded me of the day he and I were in the Carn Mòr looking for shearwaters and we came upon a cave we thought in the centre of the Carn Mòr, but upon entering, we discovered a big hole in the centre. Curiosity got the best of us so we went to explore the depth of this hole, we had between the two of us 20 yards of rope. We descended 40 yards, that's all the length of rope we had. We came to the conclusion that it appeared to us that it was a bottomless pit, we talked about our discovery to our elderly [neighbours] but as far as the answers we received from them was they never heard of it. Like many others things on the Island, that hole in Carn Mòr still remains a mystery to us. We came upon it and we did plan to return to it someday, but this never happened. It might have been a mine of some kind.

In Glean Mòr there is a river and quite a number of pools. Neil reminded me of a certain pool that always had sleek oil on the surface. The water in this pool, one could not drink it, so there is a strong possibility that oil could be found in Glean Mòr. Neil was of the belief that there is oil on that part of the Island of St Kilda. Neil was an expert at sheep raising and his wedding was the last to be performed on the Island, and no doubt the first bride to wear a white wedding gown.

Neil's wife was Finlay MacQueen's oldest daughter, who lived at No. 2 Main Street, St Kilda. Neil's wife was a great worker, she was strong and I'm sure if she was given the opportunity she could do a man's work any day, physically she was strong. As far as I can ascertain Neil was contented with his lot on the mainland. He liked forestry work and his wife Mary Ann worked with the forestry also so there was the two pay cheques coming in fortnightly, so financially, as Neil said to me, 'I have no worry in the world. At times I wish I had a smaller and a more compact house. This home is far too large for two people. The house I left in St Kilda as far as size is concerned, it would be ideal here'. Although Neil finished standard six in school, he had no interest in the post office work which his father was so much involved in. Neil was a farmer and a good one at that, as he said to me, 'I wish I had gone to Australia and taken up farming there. I believe with a little bit of luck I could have made a success of it'.

The conversation during the evening turned to his mother. He said as far as mother was concerned she never enjoyed life on the mainland. He said that his mother often said that she was far happier in St Kilda than she was in Kincardine. 'I believe', he said, 'if father and mother had settled in Lochaline, Morven along with the other St Kildians, I believe that she would have been far happier. The isolation got her: for instance my wife, father and I left every morning before 8 a.m. and did not return until close to 6 p.m.' Here she was alone, no one to have a conversation with; on the Island of St Kilda neighbours used to pop in at any moment of the day, or if you went out to fetch a pail of water you met some people on the way to the well and also coming back. So life on Hirta was one that could never get lonesome. So he went on to say, 'I believe mother died of a broken heart. She was always talking of the good life she had on the Island.' So he said the poor soul is indeed better off, his mother was a very kind and a hospitable lady, ready to help the sick and the needy. Doing this, the gracious woman was in her element.

I visited this aunt of mine when I was on leave from France in 1944 and I certainly enjoyed my stay with her. She fought a good fight, she finished her course, she kept the faith and I feel certain that the crown that she deserved was waiting for her in the home beyond the ramparts of this world. Yes, I detected that she was a lonesome woman but I tried my very best to encourage her. Regardless of the praise one would convey to her about the mainland and her present surrounding, nevertheless she was bound to finish up by saying there is no place like St Kilda; to a great extent she was expressing the truth. A nephew of hers, Malcolm MacDonald who died in 1979, was of the same nature. He too would have gladly spent his last days in his native Island, with the result that his last wish was that he be cremated and his ashes buried in the cemetery on the Island of St Kilda where he was born. I'm more than delighted that his last wish was met. Rev. Forbes from the Church of Scotland in Uist travelled with his ashes and saw them buried in the Island cemetery. His sons I understand are planning on visiting their father's birthplace and also erecting a stone on his grave in the not far distant future apparently. His aunt in Kincardine was just attached to St Kilda and I agree with her son that she died of a broken heart.

Also Neil and I got on the subject of the evacuation and what really led up to it. His version of it was this: the lack of manpower, 'At last', he said, 'we did not have enough manpower to gather the sheep to shear them, not enough manpower to go into the cliffs to harvest the fulmar. Lack of human power, so there was no other alternative but to petition the Government to have us removed to the mainland where we could make a decent living.' Also if the Government had established a regular mail service summer and winter, people would have been far more contented. 'I have no regrets', he said, 'by leaving the Island. Life no doubt was a hard one on the Island at times', he said, 'the work got beyond us, unable to do it on account of lack of help and too many vacant homes on the Island, No. 3 vacant, No. 4 vacant, No. 12 vacant and also No. 8's home'. Those mentioned at one time had large families, so this was Neil's version of the evacuation.

In Reference to the Women's Responsibility on the Island.

There is an old saying but nevertheless a true one that a woman's work is never done. Take for an example our own family, six men and one woman. On Monday morning if the weather was ideal to wash cloth and to get them dried, first thing that I noticed mother doing was to find the three legged pot and our share in the day's washing was to see that we made a trip to the well and brought home a couple of pails of water. A special fire was required to get the water to a boil then the tub was placed outside the front door. It would take mother approximately all forenoon before she would get the washing out to dry. She would have in the wash at least five white shirts, which we called Sunday shirts and all of the male family used a collar and tie, which was called Sunday best. Ironing these shirts was a chore in itself; old fashion irons that had to be heated in the fire and one had to have a good fire in order to accomplish this ironing. This took time, skill and patience.

As there were no shops on the Island where one could run out and buy a loaf of bread, mother's responsibility was to see that enough bread was available at all times. This meant that she was baking scones every day with the exception of Sunday and double had to be baked on Saturday. The St Kildians had a famous dish for their lunch on Sunday: a dumpling placed in a cloth, the three legged pot placed on the fire and left with a good fire burning when we left for the morning service at the Kirk. On our return from church the dumpling was about ready to serve. This was Sunday special and mother had to prepare this on Saturday.

In 1967 I visited Stornoway in Lewis. I had a cousin married in Lenishader Lewis. This Stornoway friend of mine took me to see her. Her husband was sick and confined to bed. As I entered the kitchen here, she was sitting by the fire knitting a pair of socks and on the fire there was a pot boiling. She was exceptionally glad to see me. She said, 'Donald, in that pot is a dumpling, the same as we used to have in St Kilda for a Sunday lunch. I make it the same way as I used to make in my beloved Island. I hope you will remain with me so that I shall be able to share it with you', and this I did. All the spinning done on St Kilda during my lifetime there was done by the women. This definitely was considered as women's work. So mother used to spin in the winter till twelve midnight, with the exception of Saturday, when work came to an end at 9 p.m. Now she would ask us had we our shoes shined. On Sunday we were allowed to wear our shoes but during the week we were sent to day school on our bare feet. Those who were in the habit of shaving, this had to be done on Saturday night. She saw that all pails were filled with water. On a hot summer Sunday if one wanted a cool drink you took a cup to the well, had your drink but you had to return home with an empty cup.

Another responsibility that belonged to women's work on Hirta was the milking of the cows. Milk, look after, saw it placed in a cool spot, and the cream placed in a churn. After school this was our chore. A homemade churn, this churn was operated by hand power, it would take approximately an hour and a half until the cream turned into butter, also making cheese and the cheese made by the St Kildian women, were of the very best. The women of the Island spent the long winter months knitting socks and gloves. The women always carried their knitting with them wherever they went, going for a bag of peats to Glean Mòr, on their way they used to knit with the result that we used to have fourteen pairs of socks and twenty-four pairs of gloves in readiness for the summer seasons. Tourists bought the socks and gloves, this meant ready cash for the household.

I heard one of the youngest girls that left the Island at the evacuation in 1930 discussing her experience trying to sell socks, gloves and egg-shells, placing, she said, 'gloves and socks over her arms and carrying a basket of egg shells, guillemot, fulmar, razorbill, puffin and gannets; these egg shells were of different colours. We were often very fortunate in selling the gloves and the egg shells'.

Flora, who was our next door neighbour on St Kilda, was a very attractive young girl and a great sales woman. She lived at No. 14 Main Street and we lived at No. 15 Main Street. One could not have better neighbours. Her mother was a widow; therefore Flora and the other sisters worked hard on the croft. Those girls helped my mother on several occasions; helped her with the washing and also with the spinning, and many other chores that required the touch of a woman's hand. I heard mother say in her younger days around the first part of May the men would take a boat to Dun where the young lambs had wintered and the lambs were removed from the Island Dun and ewes would then be driven over to Glean Mòr, where they would stay throughout the summer. The women would be responsible for milking the ewes daily. I recall mother and I on a very beautiful summer day on Glean Mòr gathering peats very near the spot where the separation of the lambs from their mothers took place; this would take place in the evening. The enclosure where the ewes were kept was built of stone; the enclosure for the lambs was of the same build. In the morning they would be led to pasture. My mother went on to say that it was the women's responsibility to keep the herd separated all day and she said this was a continual chore. The milking took place in the enclosure in the morning before they were led out to pasture. She pointed out to me the one that belonged to our family.

A woman's work on the Island was not an easy one. The week before the expedition to Boreray took place to shear the sheep, mother used to take about a week baking scones and oatcakes; butter and cheese were also made and placed in the provision box my oldest brother used to take with him. All the women on the Island found themselves just as busy as my mother, and I never saw mother consulting a paper as to the articles that should be in that box; she had a magnificent memory, even to see that salt as well as sugar was not missing. Once in on Boreray, if you didn't have [something], you could not drop in on the neighbours to borrow as you could on the Island of Hirta, as often happened.

Married women were distinguished by a white frill which they carried like a comb in the front of their head gear. During my life on the Island the women wore a plaid; various colours mostly imported from the mainland were considered very fine and worn on Sundays and special occasions with white muslin caps. I attended worship in various parts of the Highlands and I'm thoroughly convinced that the manner worship was conducted on the Island was certainly of a dignified manner as far as the Islanders were concerned. During my twenty-four years the Lord's day was the happiest day of the week, kept according to Scripture, 'Remember the Sabbath day to keep it holy', and this command was certainly adhered to when the benediction was pronounced. The women moved out of the church first, this was the custom, followed by the men and boys. The women on St Kilda were never idle.

[*The Queen's Visit and the Work of Allan Aiken*]

I heard Mary MacDonald, a daughter of William MacDonald, No. 3 Main Street when she was in grade three in the St Kilda School house one afternoon repeating the following:

If I were the Queen
What would I do
I'd sit on my throne
Eating crisps and ice cream
That's what I do
All the day long.

The teacher taught her this verse a day or two before that. This is one little girl's idea of what the Queen does, but I suspect that the Queen has more to do than sit on her throne, and that maybe she eats something other than crisps and ice cream. The Jubilee year, not only the Queen was exceptionally busy, but all the Royal family was. The present Queen is a good visitor; she visits as many parts of her realm as she is able to do. I recall her inviting all of us during her Jubilee to join her in giving thanks for the twenty-five years of her reign. Some of us may think that being Queen there is no need for her to say thank you; our Queen does not agree.

St Kilda since evacuation in 1930 hath attracted many visitors from all over the world, attracted talented men and women from various lands, artists, singers and writers. Allan Aiken [*sic*], who has led many party workers to the Island, through the years rebuilt homes and repaired *cleits*. Allan made a magnificent job of rebuilding homes and he also repaired roads. Allan has an additional reward from his St Kilda interest. He met his wife Judy, editorial assistant in the Trust's publicity department, on an early working party.

The church, even when in a state of disrepair, has now seen Christian services held by nearly every denomination, organised by the army or by parties from ships, or by members of working groups. When the Queen and Prince Philip visited St Kilda in 1971 as part of the tour of the Western Isles, according to Allan, they both expressed great interest in the renovation of the church and asked Allan many questions about it. There are hopes that the church may be reopened on an ecumenical basis and that it may welcome a royal presence. The Queen was accompanied by the Earl of Wemyss, president of the National Trust for Scotland, when she, Prince Philip, and their family visited the Island of St Kilda in the Outer Hebrides. During their stay they toured remains of a village abandoned in 1930. The picture was taken of the Royal family between Neil Ferguson's home which is No. 5 Main Street and Angus Gillies No. 6 Main Street. They are standing in the very spot where St Kilda parliament gathered every day of the week with the exception of Sunday. It must have been quite a sight, the *Britannia* in Village Bay.

The day was ideal, beautiful sunshine and the sea as calm as a pond. If the inhabitants of the Island had been there to welcome her, I can say with a certainty that the St Kildians would have received the Royal party with open arms and providing that there was not a musical instrument on the Island, I feel positive that the Islanders would have sung 'God save our gracious Queen' in English, and also in Gaelic, and I can say this as a native of the Island, she would not have left the Island empty handed. I must raise my voice and say if it was not for Allan's talents and great interest in restoring and rebuilding, St Kilda today would be a sore sight. I hope and pray that Allan will change his mind and continue to go to the Island we all St Kildians love, and continue the great work he has begun. He is essentially a team man, who has the knack of making every project a group effort, and in making each person feel that their contribution, large or small, is an important and vital one. Let us hear Bobby Peat's contribution to Allan 'as a leader of a technical working party, he is second to none, and has the happy knack of getting people to do things they are not keen on doing'.

The contribution of Archie Maynard says, 'He is modest, quiet and knowledgeable, and a first class leader'. If one asks Allan about his feelings now he says, 'It has all been a shared thing with many contributors', and on his feelings about the Island, 'It cuts one down to size on St Kilda. A small shirt fits you, as the saying has it; life there is reduced to basics, and the remoteness of the place and its beautiful clean atmosphere deeply appeals to me.'

There is a famous line of poetry, about being nearer to God in a garden; to me the Island of St Kilda has the same effect and Allan has the satisfaction of knowing that if he and his work parties had not gone to St Kilda many of the buildings would by now be ruinous heaps. The trim cottages, rebuilt walls and *cleits*, the school and the church, stand in silent tribute both to the character of the people of the past and also to the skill and enthusiasm of the new St Kildians who have given of themselves to the Islands' long story.

[*50th Anniversary of the Evacuation*]

The *Daily Record* for Friday 29th August 1980 reports as follows:

> The exiles' return coincided with the restoration of the old church on Village Bay, where a rededication service was held to mark the 50th anniversary of the evacuation.The service was taken by the Rev Donald John Gillies of Vancouver, British Columbia, Canada, who left St Kilda in 1924 at the age of 23, and fittingly one of the psalms he chose was, 'How I love this place oh God'.

I felt it quite an honour and a privilege to take part in the celebration of 1980. I graduated from the Presbyterian Theological College, Montreal in the year 1933 and was ordained to the ministry of the Presbyterian Church in Canada in Knox Presbyterian Church Carberry in July 1933. On 29th May 1935, I was married in this church to a Scotch lass who was born in Turriff, Scotland, in the year May 1911, a daughter of Mr and Mrs John Gilmore of Aberdeen, Scotland, namely Lillian Patterson Gilmore.

In the celebration of 1980 which took place in the church on St Kilda 24th August 1980 at 5 p.m. the following address was delivered:

I am pleased to be here today on this important occasion, celebrating the 50th anniversary of the evacuation of the Island, and also the re-dedication of the church, the most important building on Hirta, the House of God.

This particular spot where we find ourselves gathered today is sacred to the memory of many. It was here that they received their early education and religious training, and since have gone forth to other parts of the Empire, and for that matter, other parts of the world, and have made a mark for themselves in their new homes.

We live in a time when much of what was old and cherished is being questioned and doubted but it seems to me that there are a few matters which should be beyond dispute. The value of the great Scottish virtues: of honest pride, of self reliance, of independence of spirit, of deep religious senses of love and of education – surely these are beyond all doubts. I'm proud of the National Trust of Scotland for the marvellous effort they are putting forward in the restoration of abandoned places of great historic and religious value. All men of Scottish blood have a just pride in the land of their fathers and forefathers. No matter where they may be found, no matter what country in which they live, speak of Caledonia, land of mountains, lochs and glens, and the eye brightens, the pulse quickens and the heart thrills, with a deep love of country.

I will not attempt, as it would be utterly impossible within the compass of this short address, to narrate all the characteristics of all the people who attended divine service in this church; however, I will devote a few minutes to a description of their religious customs and practices.

The greatest event of the year was the communion service which was held during the month of July. The service commenced on Thursday and concluded Monday evening. These services continued almost without intermission, the nights being given up to prayer, praise and exhortation.

Thursday was called the day of fasting, in Gaelic *La Traisg,* and as such was literally observed by the faithful who abstained entirely from food until the afternoon, and they indulged only in light refreshments. Friday was known as the question day, *La Ceist.* After the preliminary singing and the invocation of the divine blessing, the minister called for the question.

I can recall William MacDonald, the precentor, standing here 56 years ago reading a text from the Book of Malachi, chapter 3 verse 18, 'Then shall ye return and discern between the righteous and the wicked, between him that serveth God and him that serveth Him not.'

He then asked for its interpretation, which virtually meant a differential diagnosis between saints and sinners. The minister invariably led in the discussion and, as was always the custom, the ones who opened the text for discussion also closed the service with prayer. On Saturday afternoon at the conclusion of the preaching for the day, the candidates for sacramental admission presented themselves for examination as to their knowledge of the doctrines of the Gospel, their experience of its saving power and their performance of religious duties. Many and trying were the questions put forth and answered, and sorrowful indeed was the condition of the poor person put back for another year. I have heard that this occurred in other parts of the Highlands but I never heard that it happened on this Island.

Matters reached their culmination on Sunday when the sacrament was dispensed. Slowly, the men and women, mostly past middle age, arose from their seats and proceeded to the white covered communion tables while a psalm was being sung, usually the 103rd psalm to the tune Dundee.

Nobody could gaze upon these people without being impressed by their sincerity and seriousness, with conviction that their experience was a blessed reality and not a vanishing dream. It was one of the most grand and sublime sights that one could ever behold and compelled one to think of him who preached to the multitude on the shores of Gennesaret with the ripple of the waves on the strand, as the undertone of the words of life from His lips.

The Islanders owed a great deal to the late outstanding theologian called The Apostle of the North, Rev. John MacDonald D.D. minister of Ferintosh in the Black Isle. According to what I remember discussed on many occasions by my father and grandfather, he was the first missionary in the early 19th century to bring the true message of salvation to the Island. He was also responsible for the building of this church and schoolhouse. He made four trips to the Island; on his first trip he found that he was unable to land in Village Bay and was welcomed ashore by the Islanders at North Glen. Several feet from his landing spot, he noticed a well, removed his hat and drank. A cairn was built at this spot and stands to this day, it was named 'eternal well', in the Gaelic language '*tobar na mauch*'.

The Lord's day was the happiest day of the week and kept according to the Scripture, 'Remember the Sabbath day to keep it holy', and this commandment was certainly adhered to. When the benediction was pronounced at the conclusion of the service, it was the custom that the women moved out of the church first, followed by the males.

The only elder that I can recall was my grandfather Donald Ferguson and as a speaker he was very articulate and solemn. His words were carefully chosen and he spoke from the depths of his own large experience. Grandfather Ferguson differed from the majority of Christians of his own day in regards to his attitude towards the temperance question. It was then the custom among Christians to take a glass of liquor on special occasions, whisky was considered a gift from God and all men were bound to give thanks. My grandfather was a total abstainer and as the story was told to me, upon calling on a friend's home one day, the lady of the house offered him a glass of whisky. He shook his head saying, 'There has not a glass of liquor passed my lips in fifteen years'. Taking the glass away she emptied it into a cup, remarking with more hospitality than logic, 'You can still say so'. 'No no my good lady, what I will not take from a glass neither will I take from a cup.'

After I left the Island, my father was also an elder of this church. He was not the owner of many books; I can only recall three on the shelf with the family Bible, namely the works of Boston, Pilgrim Progress and Robert MacCheyne. His own soul was fed on strong meat, and he was able to take out of his treasury things new and old. He had a powerful voice, truly a gift of God, for on one occasion it was heard over a distance of two miles and saved his life from the sea.

I was born on 29th May 1901 at 3 a.m. here in No. 15 Main Street and was spiritually born here in this very building in 1924 under the ministry of the late Mr Cameron.

I saw this church repaired in the year 1919 by two tradesmen from the Isle of Skye. The Island had been bombed by a German submarine on 15th May 1918. The third shot entered the southeast corner of the church. The previous day the missionary's wife had given birth to a baby boy, and as a result was unable to leave the manse and 67 shells passed over her head. According to the information that I received from his parents, this lad graduated as a medical missionary and was sent out to Africa by the United Free Church of Scotland. However, tragically after but a year's service he was accidentally killed while crossing a bridge.

The relationship between the civilian population and the Navy men stationed on the Island during the First World War was excellent. They took great interest in the young people, telling us about life on the mainland and the advantages we would enjoy. They painted a bright picture and we naturally became curious and interested in venturing beyond our familiar shores. So I can say that the evacuation actually began twelve years before it was finalised in the year 1930. St Kilda, since evacuation, has attracted many visitors from all walks of life, even our gracious Queen and the royal family in 1971.

In closing, I must offer a sincere thank you to Allan Aiken for his interest, effort, energy and guidance to the tireless work parties that have come to St Kilda year after year. All the buildings by now would be in ruins, but instead we see trim cottages, rebuilt walls and cleits. The school and church stand in humble pride, a silent tribute both to the character of the people of the past, but also to the skill and enthusiasm of the new St Kildians who have given of themselves to the Island's long story. Fifty years since evacuation of St Kilda, a party from Mallaig, Rhu in Dunbartonshire and also from Stornoway, three parties all told, amongst whom the following attended the commemorative service on St Kilda, fifty years since the last inhabitants were evacuated. Here are some of the names that attended the service: Mrs Morag MacDonald, 13 Seaview Terrace Stornoway, a native born and her niece Mrs Bella Deans, from Belgium, Mrs Catherine MacLeod, 8 Coulregrein and Andrew MacDonald, 5 Queensland Road, daughter and son of Mr Finlay MacDonald, 25 Nicolson Road Stornoway, an original inhabitant of St Kilda and a cousin of the MacDonalds, a Mr Donald MacLeod who has come all the way from Canada to make this trip and whose mother Mrs Annie Bella MacLeod, nee Anne B. MacDonald; she resides at 28 Westview Terrace Stornoway. HMS *Shetland* sailed from Stornoway to St Kilda with those mentioned. Other ships convey the following: in *Arakan*, Miss Cathie Gillies, Mrs Ronald Johnston, Nee Rachel Gillies, Flora Gillies, Rachel Morrison, Balvicar, Easdale, her father a native born, Rev. Donald Ferguson, a Free Church of Scotland minister, Norman Gillies and wife, Lachie MacDonald. Husband and wives accompanied also. Lachie had his wife and Rachel Johnston had her husband. A number of vessels made the trip to St Kilda, including the National Trust boat, the *Kylebhan*, with Rev. Donald MacCrae, minister of the Church of Scotland on Tarbert, Harris, Moderator of the presbytery of Harris and Uist as St Kilda parish is included in that presbytery. He conveyed greetings on behalf of the Church of Scotland and took part in the commemorative service with a Gaelic address and also a Gaelic prayer which was very appropriate. Rev. Donald John Gillies, a native of St Kilda and former minister in Vancouver, British Columbia, Canada, delivered the main address on this memorial occasion. In addition to the four boats in Village Bay that conveyed passengers to the Island to take part in this event in the history of the Island, also a helicopter landed beside the church from Headquarters, Benbecula.

To my mind I do not believe that an overflowing congregation like that ever took place in the St Kilda Kirk. During my twenty-four years on the Island I never saw the church crowded like that. I cannot find words to express my appreciation to the army personnel on St Kilda for their kindness and hospitality. It was certainly a red letter day for me. From the manse in St Kilda, I telephoned my wife in Vancouver, British Columbia, Canada. This was something I thought would never happen. I was also greatly impressed with the weather conditions that week. The programme that was planned by the National Trust administration months ahead to be carried out in the manner it was planned. I must say that prayers were answered. The Atlantic sea between the sound of Harris and St Kilda certainly cooperated.

I fully believe we should have a record of the feeling of the St Kildians that returned to their native Isle, and especially it should not be overlooked that this was done through the thoughtfulness, kindness and hospitality of the National Trust of Scotland to offer this opportunity to return to the Island on the expense of the National Trust. This was greatly appreciated by those who took advantage of it. Thanks to the Trust and God bless you for this great endeavour.

[*Morag and Mae MacDonald's Visit Back to St Kilda*]

On my first visit from Canada in the year 1937, a meeting with two small lassies living with their mother in Stornoway, namely Morag and Mae MacDonald; and just imagine the thrill it was to me to meet these two lassies after a forty-three year span, standing, gazing at the bell their father rung for many years calling the St Kildians to worship on Sunday and also Wednesday prayer week. As one of them remarked to me, many's a day father rung that bell. To my mind the recording of the *Daily Record* should not be lost on account of the authenticity of the feeling of these two sisters:

> A dream came true for two sisters who wanted to return to their Island home on the edge of the world. Morag MacDonald and Mae MacLeod were among a group of exiles who returned to St Kilda. It was in 1922 that the MacDonald family of 13 left the Island of St Kilda and were forced to leave their home because of increasing hardship. All the inhabitants of the Island gathered at the jetty and bade the family farewell and wished them God's blessings and success in all their endeavours. It was a very sad day for the Islanders as this was the first break in the community and I believe this was the first being of discontentment amongst the Islanders and hastened the hour and day of August 1930. Only eight years later came the final evacuation of the jaggy, rocky Island, 45 miles west of the Outer Hebrides and approximately 110 miles from the mainland.
>
> The last 36 remaining inhabitants were taken off and settled on the mainland but, for 58 years, Morag and Mae, both now widows and living in Stornoway, harboured the dream of returning to gaze once more on the breathtaking beauty of St Kilda. As Morag said to me, 'Let it be ever so humble, there is no place as attractive to me than my native Island of St Kilda.' And these two sisters did not overlook the fact of rendering thanks to a combined effort by the Army, Navy and the National Trust for Scotland. The sisters and six other exiles once more returned to the Island of their birth.
>
> As they stepped ashore, many of the exiles openly wept and even the Atlantic which frequently lashes the Island was calm. Mrs MacDonald, now 64, of 13 Seaview Terrace, Stornoway, I asked her, 'How do you feel to set foot on the Island you first

saw the light?' She said, 'Words cannot describe how I feel; my late brother who is buried here used to say this was a far better place than any other on earth, despite the hardships, and there were many, and I agree with him. There was never any fighting or crime on St Kilda. There was a community spirit, everybody used to help each other. There was no squabbling, and we all got on so well together. Life used to be just lovely on this Island, despite the terrible winter storms.' Their special mission to the Island was to visit their brother Malcolm's grave and also to attend the rededication of the church, and also to meet other exiles who gathered there for this special occasion, and it was a reunion, meeting other natives from other parts of the country, some from Oban, Glasgow, Belgium, Ontario Canada and also from Vancouver, British Columbia. As far as the natives of the Island were concerned, it could be put down as a red letter day.

Allow me to look at St Kilda abandoned. The fishery cruiser *Harebell* brought the natives of St Kilda to the Scottish mainland. Eight families were disembarked at Lochaline pier in Morven, where forestry work on the Ardtornish estate awaits them, and the remainder continued to Oban. This completed the evacuation of the rocky Island and with its companions Soay and Boreray, stands as a lonely and storm smitten sentinel in the remotest west. The operation was desired by the St Kildians for economic reasons and from every modern point of view was wise. Nevertheless it has not been without its almost epical moments of emotion. A portion of the earth, howsoever forbidding it be, is not abandoned by all its inhabitants on one day without a deep stirring of the heart and the imagination. We can respond sympathetically to the genuine emotions which filled the heart of the St Kildians as they gazed from the deck of the Harebell at the Cone of Connacher, and the jagged peak of Boreray receding and finally vanished under the horizon. There was regret that the wild crags will test the strength of the egg gatherers no more, that the tiny fields will be forever untilled, that the bell will call no worshippers to church on Sundays, that the small boats will put out for Boreray no more and that smoke has vanished from the hearths in the straggling village. The Island has been left to the fulmars and gannets, and the surrounding waters to the whales and seals. A heritage of Pelagian existence has been broken after enduring for a thousand years, and St Kilda enters into the company of desert Islands.

The regrets aroused throughout Scotland by the evacuation are natural enough, but there is no excuse for the sort of sentiment that prompts people to argue that the Island is as fit a place for human habitation as it ever was; such a suggestion is without foundation in reality. For the past seventy years and more the primitive economic life of the St Kildians has been in process of decay and sooner or later the *Harebell* or a successor would have had to perform its affecting task. The irregular visits of trawlers and steamers brought the call of the mainland and the wider world to the youth of the wild Isles, and the response has been such that during the past few years the manpower has been so depleted as to prevent necessary work from being undertaken. Contact with modern civilisation also accustomed the natives to a rather higher standard of living than was known to their bird-catching and pastoral forebears, and lately they had come to be in some measure dependent on state aid. Their primitive Gaelic mode of living in fact had come to an end and the issue was one of life in new hopeful and honourable circumstances or of a decrepit and anachronistic existence unlit by any gleam of hope. The rejuvenation of St Kilda's economic resources was well nigh beyond human powers, and the elementary type of existence alone possible on her meagre meadow land served no purpose either cultural, economic, or genetic in the corporate life of the state. Evacuation was the only possible course open to the Islanders and the authorities. To harbour regret therefore, would be to blind one's eyes to the facts. The St Kildian village community has now passed out of existence and its surviving representatives have been launched upon a new life in new surroundings, with every good wish and much practical help at their disposal. The St Kildians proved to be capable of adjusting themselves to the tasks before them. Many of the Islanders at one time or another paid visits to the mainland, therefore finding themselves among new environments and it did not take long to adjust to any situation that came to them. Leaving the Island was an excellent move especially for the rising generation. I interviewed several young Islanders who left the Island in 1930 and the following is their reaction and all of them with one voice uttered: 'We have no regrets that we left the Island.'

The present day St Kildians, while still clinging to their heritage as Islanders in a remote and isolated community, much prefer the life they lead now. Mr Norman Gillies and a nephew of mine, here is what he had to say, 'I'm extremely pleased to find myself on the mainland, where I'm established in a good job. I was only five years old when I left St Kilda in 1930. I moved first to Morven and was educated in that area at the outbreak of the Second World War'. He joined the Navy and served with great distinction and he was honourably discharged at the end of hostility, returned to Morven for a very short period of time and then returned to England to Ipswich, where he is a manager of a wallpaper and paint store. He married a native of Chelmsford and established a home and called it St Kilda House. He is also very active in the church. His family consists of two girls and a boy. Here is one that made well and he truly can say for him and his family, it was God's blessing that the evacuation of 1930 took place.

It was Norman John's mother, Mrs Mary Gillies, who brought the evacuation plans to a head at a time when the Islanders and the authorities were still arguing over them. She became ill with appendicitis in 1930, but it was more than a month before she could be taken off the Island by boat to be transferred to a Glasgow hospital, where she died soon after. The Islanders took her death badly and decided that evacuation was the only method of survival for most of them. All the St Kildians I had the opportunity to talk with since leaving the Island, the answer was unanimous, 'we have no regrets; we are far better off here on the mainland'.

[*The Last Mail Leaving St Kilda*]

One of the first essential things to be seen secured was the Registration Examiner of the northern district. A Mr Ross was responsible for this and he was the first to land, all the official records were removed and taken on the steamship, which also took on board the last mail to leave the Island. This was the heaviest known in the history of the Island and the ingoing mail was the lightest. The previous ingoing mail included requests to the postmaster from all parts of the country for souvenirs such as lengths of the famous St Kilda Tweed, snaring rods, stuffed birds and St Kilda wool. Some people enclosed postal orders with the request that the postmaster should send heather or fragments of rock if nothing better could be obtained.

> The *Dunra Castle* left at midday for the last time Village Bay with the siren blowing and the Islanders waving farewell. There was little more to be done and it is expected that HMS *Harebell* will be ready to take the St Kildians to the mainland tonight. The *Dunra Castle* is making for Oban where the Islanders' livestock will be landed. It is worthy to notice that the Islanders were compelled to leave 300 sheep on Boreray, the neighbouring Island. A recent expedition found the sheep so wild that barely a score were captured.

It was rumoured that two wanted to remain on the Island, namely Neil Ferguson, my uncle, and his wife. I talked to my uncle about this and his answer was that this story was untrue. His son Neil Ferguson, age 72, was one of the few St Kildians who has been back to the Island since the evacuation.

'I was depressed', he said, 'to see the carcasses of sheep lying, even in the church where we used to worship. As a young man of 30, I was glad to leave St Kilda, and as an old man I am now not sorry that I had to leave.' His father and mother lived in the same home in Kincardine. His mother was always lonesome for St Kilda and Neil, her son, maintained that she died from a broken heart.

There is a strong possibility that if they had settled in Morven with the rest of the Islanders, no doubt she would have been happier.

Neil's father was postmaster and postman; I can recall seeing him delivering mail to each resident. In addition to this, he was the only elder in the Kirk and he had to officiate in the absence or illness of the missionary; not only had he to take the pulpit on Sunday but also he was the school manager who signs the register and at times he had to conduct examinations. He was also the ground officer representing the estate which let the grazings, was also responsible for Soay and he was the one who permitted the Islanders to go and kill so many sheep for their own consumption. As many of the Islanders could not read, speak or write English, many's a letter he wrote for those who found themselves in that category. All in all I can truly say that the Islanders also depended upon him for sound advice. He was a very remarkable man in every sense of the word.

He died in Kincardine as he entered the Church of Scotland on Sunday morning, a church he was an elder in. Death came very sudden and unexpected and knowing him as I did, for him it was to die is gain. It certainly could be said of him: 'Well done good and faithful servant'.

[*My First Visit to St Kilda in 1966*]

My first visit to the Island I was born on was 1966. What a change I discovered, a change and a sight to behold, some things that I never expected to see on the Island. It never dawned on me as a youngster, going to school barefooted and very often carrying a peat along with my books under my arm, that one day I would land ashore in a landing craft on the beautiful sandy beach of the loveliest Island in the Hebrides, St Kilda, and this happened. To be conveyed to Mullach Mhòr in a truck was also an unbelievable occurrence and also seeing a helicopter landing not too far from the church on the manse property, delivering mail and groceries to the army kitchen, and it only took 30 minutes from Benbecula to St Kilda. This sight I never expected to see.

Also I observed empty oil drums and the noise of heavy army transport that I'm afraid would cause the early St Kildians to vibrate, if not turn in their graves. I never expected to see a pub on the Island during my lifespan, nevertheless I saw this. Whoever thought of the name of the pub to my mind ought to be congratulated, for one could not find a better and more suitable than to be called the Puffin's Inn. As I stood at the door of the cottage I was born in, I started wandering to my early childhood. I immediately came to the conclusion there was little or no comparison between the life-style of the present occupants and that of the original Islanders. Undoubtedly I discovered that there was every comfort and luxury provided for the army, including adequate transport by sea and air if required and, may I say this, that's how it should be. The army personnel deserves the very best, as one who served with the 21st Canadian Armour Regiment, as protestant chaplain and saw service in Holland and finished at Williams Haven on Armistice day. The army personnel on St Kilda, I wish them every comfort and God's richest blessing on all their endeavours.

However, I thought, how does this compare with the hardships which were suffered by the original local inhabitants and myself included, rock climbing, crofters and fishermen, who for generations battled against the elements until they were finally obliged to accept evacuation to the mainland? One of the contributing factors that they could not be guaranteed was the necessary supplies being delivered by sea, owing to the severe gales in the winter which cut off the Islands. It seems to me that the powers to be did the magnificent thing to accept the request of the thirty inhabitants to be removed to the mainland, providing that the Government would have offered the luxury that the army is enjoying on St Kilda at the present time. It would be impossible for the thirty people to survive on account of the hard way that living had to be provided, since there wasn't sufficient manpower left. I say this on account of the hardship I experienced on the Island in my twenty-four years living there.

Two passenger steamers that were well known to the St Kildians were SS *Hebrides* and the SS *Dunra Castle*. In the year 1932 the death of Captain John MacKinnon of the *Hebrides*, which took place at his home in Glasgow, removed a notable figure from the west coast Highland Coasting Trade. Captain MacKinnon was master of the vessel for about eleven years, having succeeded the late Captain John Campbell in January 1921, and for several years prior to that he had been chief officer of the same vessel. He in fact served the full period of his seafaring career, about forty years, which he gave to the West Highland Coasting Trade, in the same company's vessel starting at the lowest rung of the ladder till he got command of the *Hebrides*, having thus been on the same route during his whole seafaring career. He was well known practically in every port of call on the west coast, as well as to the tourists who in the course of that long period had taken their passage in his vessel while visiting St Kilda. His vessel and his own familiar figure were always eagerly watched for by the natives of the Lone Isle when it was inhabited, and they all knew and adored Captain MacKinnon. He endeared himself to the Islanders who travelled in his vessel to parts of the Outer Hebrides to visit friends and most of these elderly people could not talk English but Gaelic and MacKinnon was able to converse with them in this language as he was a very fluent Gaelic speaker. As the Islanders took a steerage passage as they could not afford anything any better, Captain MacKinnon often invited the St Kildians to his own quarters in the *Hebrides*. My father visited me in Glasgow in 1926 and he couldn't praise Captain MacKinnon enough for his kindness and hospitality to him during his journey from St Kilda to Glasgow. He was a native of the Island of Coll, of which Island his predecessor Captain Campbell was also a native. Captain Campbell was also well thought of and liked by all who came in contact with him; he too could speak the language of the Island, Gaelic.

[*My Last Trip on the SS Hebrides in 1937*]

My last trip on the SS *Hebrides* was in 1937, the year of the coronation of King George the Sixth. Mrs Gillies and I left at the end of May from Sydney, Cape Breton, Nova Scotia, Canada on the SS *Nova Scotia*, a passenger ship that journeyed from Boston USA to Halifax and Sydney, Nova Scotia, and the last port of call was St Johns, Newfoundland, bound for Liverpool, England. This was my first visit from Canada since emigrating to Canada in the year 1927. As the SS *Hebrides* was still making trips to St Kilda with tourists, I met the SS *Hebrides* on this occasion in Lochmaddy, with the intention of making the trip to the Island. Normally, weather permitting, they usually sail directly from Lochmaddy to the Island of St Kilda, but on this trip on account of the wind being from the southeast, a wind which directly sweeps into Village Bay, the SS *Hebrides* made for Tarbert.

The captain, and I cannot recall his name, who knew that I was a native of the Island and anxious to visit it, came to me after he landed on Tarbert, Harris, and informed me of the bad news on account of the direction of the wind. He said, 'I am afraid that I shall be unable to land tomorrow on the Island', and as I was intending to visit Stornoway he advised me that it would be better for me to disembark on Tarbert, Harris, and continue my journey to Stornoway by bus, so this I did. Naturally I was greatly disappointed coming all the way from Canada and not able to land on Hirta, but we have no control over the stormy seas of the Atlantic Ocean. The One who controls the wind and the storm is the One who was with the disciples in a boat on the lake of Galilee, and being weary lay down and slept. A storm arose, the wind and waves boisterous, the disciples arrived at the panic stage so at last they woke Him. He stood in the boat, looked at the angry waves and uttered 'peace be still' and immediately a great calm took place.

On my return from Stornoway to Larachbeg, Morven, I recall my brother Donald relating the dreaded south easter sweeping into Village bay on the last trip of the SS *Hebrides*, a few days before the evacuation took place. The *Hebrides* landed the tourists as usual by the St Kildian small boats, charging each passenger a shilling to ferry them ashore and also that shilling covered their ferry back to the ship. On this particular occasion the passengers were only ashore barely two hours when the steamer whistled, a signal that all must return to the ship. The weather conditions had changed in the short time the passengers were on the Island.

My brother related that the wind which had been fresh from the south during the morning and all of sudden the wind changed to the southeast. That's the worst wind for Village Bay. Apparently some of the Islanders were of the opinion that it was too dangerous to ferry the passengers to the SS *Hebrides.* All the passengers were standing on the stone jetty, hearing the Islanders talking Gaelic and wondering what was going to take place. Instead of making an attempt to ferry the passengers, here the Islanders began to haul their boats maintaining that it was too risky to attempt to reach the ship with a cargo of human beings. The ship's captain was at a loss wondering what was taking place on the shore. Were they going to attempt ferrying the passengers to the *Hebrides* or what was going on? At last the missionary on the Island, a Mr Munro who was a Navy man, communicated with the ship's captain what was taking place. When the captain discovered this, he ordered the boats to be launched from the vessel. When the Islanders discovered this, they made the attempt and with great struggle managed to ferry all passengers to the ship.

My brother continued by saying the sight of the ship's boats being lowered came as a shock to the Islanders; this was the first time within living memory of the Islanders that something like this ever happened. The boat that my brother Donald manned had seven passengers and eight Islanders, 'and with that we set out for the ship. The journey, about six hundred yards, took the better part of thirty minutes. While it lasted it was most exciting, the waves by this time mountainous and the eight oarsmen, two to each oar, fought every inch of the way, the oars bending under the terrific strain put upon them.' 'Half way out', he continued to say, 'We were as close to being swamped as ever I care to be. An incautious movement of the tiller brought our boat nearly broadside to the foaming breaking crest of a great green mountain of water and the water dashed over us. The ship side reached, the passengers boarded by each jumping as the boat rose to the top of the wave to be caught by the willing hands of the crew. That was the worse southeast storm I ever experienced ferrying passengers to their ship. That last visit of the SS *Hebrides* before evacuation cannot be easily forgotten.'

The cottage I lived in, No. 15 Main Street, and all the other cottages are the same size, three-roomed and, to my mind, far above the standard of the black houses on many of the Hebridean Islands. I can say that the fulmar was a favourite dish with us, caught before it's capable of flying. The killing of the young fulmar began on 3rd August and this slaughter continued until each family had two full barrels salted (some bigger families required two and half barrels at least), a barrel of salted mutton also along with half a barrel of fish, cod, ling and bream. The head of the family saw that he had this much for consumption during the winter month. The St Kildians weave or knit all their own clothes, rough tweeds and jerseys.

Each cottage is fronted by a fair sized [word omitted?]. No rates or taxes paid, the rent is nominal and medical help and education is free. As far as medical aid is concerned, many a year the Island was left without even a nurse provided. The factor of the Island built a lovely modern house for a nurse to be stationed there. One often asks the questions why were the Islanders so anxious to leave their native Island in 1930 and great many answers have come forward. I would say without hesitation or shadow of a doubt the following were at least some contributing factors, one is the sickness of isolation and the lack of manpower. St Kilda is without mail from October to February and sometimes even to the month of May, except by the kindness of trawlers. She is cut off from the outside world, her young people are restive, there is not nowadays the fear and doubt of the mainland which assailed an earlier generation. Personally, I only discovered two individuals who have not been away from the Island on a visit, namely one is Mrs MacDonald, widow of Donald MacDonald, who lives at No. 16 Main Street, and the other her daughter, a widow Mrs Neil Gillies, who lives at No. 7 Main Street. Finlay MacQueen, the oldest Islander, had a trip to the mainland. Finlay owns 200 sheep and was in his day one of the finest cragsmen in Britain. He still descends the great cliffs for fulmar using sixty fathom ropes. Finlay drives in a peg and descends alone; he was an expert at this, a fearless man. He was a very heavy pipe smoker, and when Finlay was out of tobacco, he wasn't in the very best of moods. Without tobacco he inclined to be cranky, nevertheless he was kind and very considerate.

On my first visit to St Kilda in 1966 in an army landing craft that came from Rhu in Dumbarton Scotland, the first stop was Benbecula in Uist, where we took in more supplies for the army on the Island who are manning the radar station. I was looking forward to this nostalgic visit, going through the sound of Harris it was like a millpond. However we weren't very far on the journey until I heard the foghorn, surely the most mournful note to chill the heart of any mariner. I went on deck and made my way to the bridge. From the bridge I could barely discern the bow, and very disappointing the weather forecast offered no hope of any change. The north Atlantic was blanketed with thick white fog of the type much beloved by film makers when telling the story of Jack and Gill that went up the hill to fetch a pail of water but for film makers that were with us on this particular journey who were trying to capture the soaring outlines of St Kilda, it was no consolation to hear from the ship's crew that they had never experienced such conditions in the six years' experience of the St Kilda run. On the bridge I peered through the fog, sometimes imagining that I was seeing Islands looming ahead. I still recall the words of the captain to myself and the film makers, 'You will never see anything looking out at eye level, you got to look up'. Pointing up there, his hand was pointing almost straight up. Dutifully, we all raised our eye level and quite suddenly out of the whiteness planed a gannet, surely the most graceful of all seabirds. Then there was another and another and suddenly the sky was full of them, hundreds of these silent birds, wheeling around us.

I suppose that we all saw the peak of the stack rising out of the fog at the same moment. It was Stac Lee, black and jagged towering out of the sea and then we saw Stac an Armin and Boreray, the landscape of dreams. On the sea there were rafts of puffins; then the fog closed in again and all of us were left wondering if we had imagined the whole thing.

There is no such place as St Kilda. The story goes that a careful map maker wrote on his chart not only the Gaelic word *tobar*, which means a well, but also its equivalent in Old Norse *childe*. What he really wrote was in fact, 'well: well'. As Scotland has a long tradition of dedicating wells to saints, it was thought that this well on the lonely Island in the Atlantic was dedicated to a saint called 'childe' or 'Kilda'. There is no such saint in any hagiography, but the name stuck and is applied to the group of Islands consisting of Hirta, Boreray, Dun, Soay, Stac Levenish, Stac an Armin and Stac Lee, as well as some dark needles of rock, such as Stac Birroch, near Soay. I have heard other versions of how the name St Kilda came about but I'm inclined to favour this one. The tiny Island of Hirta is truly stupendous; it is almost two dimensional like a stage setting for a Wagner opera. Five peaks soar into the mists, none smaller than 900 ft. Conachair rises to almost 1400 ft, its cliffs dropping sheer to the sea.

The fog cleared and we landed on the sand beach of St Kilda. On that occasion walking through the stones of the ruined homes, the fanks and *cleits*, to be honest I was overwhelmed by the sadness of the place. I have never seen a ghost although I heard some natives on the Island claiming that they did. A native, Ewen Gillies, passing No. 11 one night, he saw two men passing him. He did not recognise them but in three weeks after that the tragic drowning at the Dun took place when two brothers were lost and not even the bodies were discovered. This was supposed to be the two Ewen saw passing him. Reading in the good Book the story of Jesus walking on the sea, the disciples were in a small boat and they saw a man walking on the sea. They thought, the story goes on to tell us, that they saw a ghost. Whether the St Kildians took it from that story, this I never know, but truthfully on that trip to Hirta, I sensed and heard the spirit of the place mourning among the ruins and I'm still haunted by the memory of the Island that trip.

As I have mentioned ghosts, I can recall this story and mind you these types of stories made you nervous. I often ran fast past that bit of the road that led up to the cemetery gate. I heard so many queer stories of something that natives saw as forerunner of funerals. There was a widower living alone and this particular afternoon I was with my uncle who was putting hinges on our barn door. I was about ten years old, and about three in the afternoon my aunt was in the house alone and we saw this neighbour of ours going in at our front door. He only lived up the road, I suppose five minutes walk, and while my uncle was putting away his tools I went into the house. I looked into the one room kitchen and there was no sign of the man and I called to my aunt, who was in the bedroom doing a little bit of sewing. Oh she got kind of cross with me, said 'This man is not here at all'. So my uncle came in and he asked me where this man was, 'he is not here', 'I saw him he must be here'. He called to auntie and she came out of the bedroom and assured my uncle that the man wasn't in the house, but the St Kildians had an old belief if you saw a man like that, that he was dead, he had dropped dead. Well they sent me over to the house to see. You talk about anybody being scared; I went into the kitchen and just sat down long enough to see the old chap there in his usual place smoking his pipe. He figured I came for something and didn't want to ask for it. So I took off for my uncle's home as fast as ever I could. I told them and they hardly believed me that he was alright, but that man only lived two weeks after that. That took place on a Friday, seeing him entering my uncle's home, and strange to say, he was buried on a Friday at about 3 p.m.; so it was the forerunner of his funeral. The natives did believe in seeing unnatural things, which they took as warning that a tragic thing would happen in the very near future. I heard my aunt saying, if you wished yourself in such and such place, it was an awful bad thing to wish that I was here or there because sometimes people had done that and something had happened to them.

There was a telephone wire stretched from the manse that's beside the stone landing jetty to Mullach Mhòr and this was used by the native watchmen. During the First World War people were seeing lights resting on this which was very unusual. However when John MacDonald, No. 9 Main Street, and Ewen Gillies, No. 12 Main Street, met death the first day of the fulmar harvest the news came by telephone from Mullach Mhòr that they were missing, and feared dead. Those who had seen the light resting on this line believed that this was a forerunner of death.

There was something else I often heard father and mother discussing, that is hearing a hen crowing before the midnight hour; they consider this as a sign of death in that family. Hens were housed in the barns in the winter and the barns are so close to the homes and in the silence of the night to hear the hen crowing brought sadness to that home, waiting patiently as to what would happen next and in every instance death within a short period of time took place in that home or in a relative's home.

Rèiteach, a Scottish Engagement Rite

I remember three weddings taking place in the St Kilda church in the evening round 6 p.m., my brother Donald, John MacDonald, and Neil Gillies in the year 1916. I was a lad of fifteen years then. A *rèiteach* is said to be an espousal held before the banns of marriage are proclaimed and is sometimes considered as important as the wedding feast itself, but that is a later definition. If a man happens to be out in the field removing stones, if you asked his wife what he was busy at she might tell you in Gaelic, '*Tha e trang aig obair rèiteach*'. I imagine that word '*rèiteach*' comes from the word for settling things, clearing out obstacles or making the ground tillable. It was a formal way of asking for a young girl's hand, clearing the ground for a wedding, and probably questions of dowry, where the couple would live, making certain that every one involved was satisfied with the arrangements. It was very important in the preservation of family and community. It seems to be that this was the last practice of this type of celebration that took place on the Island of St Kilda. Over the years, what must have been a very rich tradition gradually wore away, until only the barest outlines of *rèiteach* were left.

It must have been at one time quite a performance. It was for some reason never held on a Friday. The bridegroom to be and an older friend, someone respected in the community, would come to the home of the girl he hoped to have for a bride. The father would usually know why they had come but it was customary that absolutely nothing would be said outright. Instead they would pretend they had come to buy a cow or a boat and beating about the bush, as the old saying has a double meaning, if it was a boat they were claiming they wanted to buy, they would ask such a question as, is she broad in the beam? Eventually they would get down to talking about the real purpose of the visit and when the older friend had finished speaking well of the bridegroom to be and asking for a certain girl's hand, the father would then go through the formality of first offering his other daughters; sometimes in fact the offering was quite serious as he perhaps wanted to marry off a particular daughter and would actually refuse to give up the girl the young man had come for. This, however, never happened on the Island of St Kilda.

This type of ceremony took place in 1916 and that was the end of the *rèiteach* as far as the Island of St Kilda was concerned. I believe that three weddings took place on the Island at the end of hostility of the First World War; a Navy chaplain married a Mary MacDonald, a daughter of Malcolm MacDonald and his late wife who lived at No. 8 Main Street. She married a Navy man by the name of MacLean, a resident of Port Glasgow. A brother of mine, John, was married quietly at the home of Mrs MacKinnon, No. 11 Main Street, to a Mary MacQueen, who lived at No. 10 Main Street, and the last wedding to take place on the Island was a first cousin of mine, Neil Ferguson, who married the oldest daughter of the famous cragsman Finlay MacQueen, who resided at No. 2 Main Street. This wedding was also quite an event, as a matter of fact the first white wedding that took place on the Island of St Kilda and also the last one. Now, for those weddings, a *rèiteach* never took place.

The *rèiteach* that took place at No. 13 Main Street in the year

1916, great preparations were made: a couple of sheep would be slaughtered for the occasion, the women of the Island found themselves baking bannocks, for weeks churning to have butter and on this special occasion there would be a glass of whisky for the purpose of proposing a toast. A big long table was prepared for a little feast, if I remember rightly this was how it was set up; at the commencement of the feast a Gaelic grace was said by the station missionary on the Island.

To my mind on this occasion it was more of a prayer than grace, and everyone except the young girl sat at the table. Her chair was left empty at the table and the young man who wished to marry her had brought an older man to speak for him. At this one I remember well that it was Neil Ferguson, my uncle the postmaster of St Kilda, that spoke at this gathering and it was all in Gaelic and he spoke I would say at least for 15 minutes. He described the future groom's qualities and love for the girl and asked for her hand and when all other arrangements were made as the final act of agreement, the young girl came to the table and sat. A glass of whisky was available, and the feast was served.

The evening of the wedding, there was absolutely no feast or celebration of any description. I remember after the church wedding, the married couple were allowed about an hour to get to bed. The only honeymoon on St Kilda, the whole inhabitants visited the couple and wished them well. This was called bedded the married couple. This custom also disappeared after 1916. The weddings that took place on the Island after that, the bedded custom had vanished. There was no dancing after celebration like this on St Kilda on account of not having any musical instruments. I believe that I had in my own possession a mouth organ that I got from one of the tourists that visited St Kilda on the SS *Hebrides*.

In the year 1937 I found myself in a Gaelic congregation called North River and North Shore in Victoria County, Cape Breton, Nova Scotia, people who I could easily compare with the life on the Island of St Kilda. Each family in my Cape Breton congregation had a croft, a couple of cows and a few sheep. In addition to this they had a small boat for fishing. However, one of my Gaelic precentors told me the following story in reference to the *rèiteachs*, a Scottish engagement rite.

He told me the following story of a man who was to be married and sometime after the *rèiteach* the girl jilted him. But the young men of the neighbourhood were determined to have a wedding, as well as the fine party that would certainly follow. So they planned a scheme for him another night to ask for the hand of a girl he never met and here in Gaelic and then English is the story, and a hint of the happy life that followed. In quite a number of cases it might be the first time the groom had ever seen the prospective wife, and in a lot of instances it wasn't a very happy episode for the girl, but it turned out quite happily after that for most of them. This man went on to say, 'I know of one particular case.' He said he wasn't there but he knew the people involved. It happened the girl had never seen the man brought before her this particular night for the *rèiteach*. This man had got the marriage garb to marry another woman and she had jilted him. It was the custom then that the man bought the apparel for his wife to be married in, along with his own. He went on to say that he did not know whether this woman returned the cloth or did she get married in it to another fellow. Anyway she left this man but the young fellows wanted to have the wedding, by hook or by crook.

There was one fellow in the group who was a planner and a schemer. This man said they'd take the man to his sister and they got a bottle or two of whisky. He wasn't sure of the number that went on this expedition. The girl had never seen the man because he was quite a bit older and she lived a distance of 6 miles from him. This man was more or less a little more prominent citizen of the community, and the parents were quite willing to look at the matter in that light. The girl was taken by surprise and she cried her heart out that night, but this man continued to say that he heard her relating the story years after to the women at a carding and spinning frolic; speaking in the Gaelic language, she said 'in the final analysis, after all the discontent of that first night, they had eight children together', and she said, 'Do you know that I never let one of them sleep one night between my husband and I.' I never heard that anything of this nature ever happened in my native Island and I'm sure from what I saw taking place on the Island of St Kilda in 1916, this took place on the Island long before this, and I feel confident all weddings that took place on the Island had a *rèiteach* and a feast before the wedding; it was then the custom of the day.

My mother in Lochaline was telling me about the two shepherds, their dogs and a representative of the Department of Agriculture to assist in the completion of the transportation of the sheep. Also left behind were about a dozen cats, whether these were left because it was thought they would do better on St Kilda or whether they were semi-wild and could not be caught. Apparently a party of naturalists arrived in July 1931; they found only three left. These presented a serious threat to the survival of the unique St Kilda house mouse and St Kilda wren, and two were shot and the third escaped. This party of naturalists found that six of the former residents had returned for the summer to weave more St Kilda tweed, among them Finlay MacQueen, the greatest without a shadow of doubt, of St Kilda cragsmen. Finlay was quite an old man by 1930 and had gone to Kincardine on Forth.

The tradition of the St Kilda cragsmen has gone and most of the men have gone too. Life, it seems to me, proved too much for man upon that wee rockie in ye western sea. To quote my brother and his wife's feelings about the place aptly, 'No I don't wish to remember anything of it, that's a life that is gone. If anyone wishes to see St Kilda they should go there but that won't tell them of all our hardships long ago.' This was the feeling of Mrs Gillies. 'Ay', said her husband, 'I have never been back and I never wish to.' Mother was the last to leave the home I was born in. I saw a picture of this scene; the spinning wheel was the last piece of furniture removed from the home. This she carried proudly to the jetty stone, placed aboard the ship's lifeboat that took it eventually to Larachbeg in Morven, Argyllshire, Scotland.

1st August 1927, serving a large rural congregation of North River and North Shore, Victoria County, Cape Breton, Nova Scotia, also called the Highlands of Cape Breton, a member of the congregation that I was serving invited me to go out fishing with him. This invitation I accepted gladly. It was a beautiful day, the sea calm and the sun hot. One could not wish for anything any better. There was an Island which was actually a bird sanctuary as no human being was living on it. As we drew close to it I got the surprise of my life: the first bird that I saw on a rock was a puffin, something that I never expected. Seeing the puffin made me lonesome. I was of the opinion that the puffin could not be seen anywhere but on St Kilda. This to my mind was the first animal to greet me to Canada.

[*The Puffin*]

The puffin is sometimes known as the sea parrot, because of its distinctive bill which in the nesting season takes on a vivid colours of red, blue, grey and ivory, receding when the nesting season ends. Winters are spent at sea but no one is sure just where. The St Kildians were of the impression that this bird emigrated to a warmer climate. As a general rule, it left the cliffs of St Kilda at the end of August for two weeks. On the west of the Island of St Kilda and directly opposite Carn Mhòr for a couple of weeks the sea would be covered with puffins (or sometimes the natives called them by a nickname, namely Tomy Norrie) for miles and miles. It was certainly a sight to behold. The largest Canadian colonies are found on Islands off Newfoundland, one of which is occupied by an estimate of 400,000 puffins. The nest is actually a burrow, which the bird digs into soft turf, slopes for a distance of about 3 feet and in which one egg is laid. The puffin is an expert swimmer and often emerges from an underwater foray with six or more small fish dangling from its serrated bill. They suffer considerable losses from herring and other gulls whose numbers are increasing due to human effluence. The puffin barbecued tasted delicious and the feathers were used for pillows.

I saw a picture of tourists on the Island of Dun who were bird watchers and they are watching puffins, the bird adopted by the St Kilda Club as their emblem. The St Kilda Club came into being in 1958 and now has over 200 members. A friend of mine, Alex Warrick, was the first president of it, a man greatly qualified for such a position. I heard Alex giving a lecture on the Island of St Kilda aboard the Uganda on one of the National Trust cruises, and believe me he was excellent describing the lone Isle of St Kilda. As a matter of fact his knowledge and interest in the Island was magnificent. I'm also glad that there is no back entry membership; it has to be earned. A member has to have stayed overnight on the Islands, none too easy a qualification when one considers distance, the uncertainty of the sea, and the perils of seasickness. Thirty people attended the first annual dinner and they chose as their badge the puffin, the perky clown like bird that lives in such large numbers on St Kilda, Soay, Boreray, Stac an Armin and Dun.

The natives had three choices in catching the puffin: first a big bamboo rod with a horsehair loop; an experienced cragsman knew how to use the rod and snare. This had to be done in a very quiet manner and you would have also to hide behind a rock that was adjacent to the rock that had 100 puffins resting. I used this method and it was workable, but you had also to take the wind into consideration. The second method was laying a trap on the stone with an anchor on it; we used to trap a great many in that way also. The third method was to use the dog and he would find the hole where the puffin had laid his egg or at the beginning of the season, mating time, you could find two in the same hole. Boreray and Soay were the two places that lent itself to this method; the holes were easy to reach on account of them being under the turf.

Brother Neil's Contribution – His Experience as a Bird Watcher on the Island of his Birth

Being a native of St Kilda and thoroughly acquainted with the Island I was selected by the agents of its present proprietor, the Earl of Dumfries, to watch his interests during the summertime and the tourist season.

St Kilda was evacuated by its inhabitants on 29th August 1930 and every summer since then I was sent out by the first tourist steamer to call at the Island and remain there till its last visit of the season.

My duties were to guard the proprietor's property from wanton destruction by souvenir hunters, and preserve the bird life which is as varied as it is numerous. It is the wish of the proprietor who is a keen ornithologist that St Kilda should be preserved as a bird sanctuary and his instructions were strictly carried out. Being a trade man I also occupied my time in keeping the housing property in repair.

The need of someone in my capacity was proved by the invasion of foreign fishermen who, in 1931, pillaged all the native houses, broke open their doors, and helped themselves to ropes, fishing gear, spinning wheels and all useful articles left by the people in their hurried exodus from the Island. Ropes and fishing lines were indispensable to the people when there, the former for climbing cliffs, and the latter for catching cod, ling and halibut, which at one time were plentiful around the Island. All those things were left behind because they were not to be of any use to them in their new vocation on the mainland under the Ministry of Forestry. Only articles of clothing and bedding, with a selection of their furniture, were removed by the emigrants. The obsolete lot was replaced by more modern articles for their new homes at Lochaline, Kincardine, Black Isle, Inverness and Culross.

During the early part of Summer since the evacuation I was accompanied on the Island by another native, Mr A. G. Ferguson, my uncle, and two handloom weavers who were anxious that their hands would not lose their cunning in weaving the famous St Kilda tweed.

I also had my mother staying with me for a month but their duties on the mainland made them all leave me in July. So I was left all alone on the deserted Island for fully three weeks, out of touch with any other human being. I was apt to start at the sound of my own voice, but my winged companions were with me night and day, cheering me with their crones [*sic*] by night and their songs by day. There was also the perpetual beating and lapping of the waves against the shores and breakers, intensified by the Atlantic swell breaking on the sand.

There is a quarter of a mile of beautiful sand there during the summer, but all is washed away by the winter billows. It was altogether a glorious experience and one which afforded food for thought, an ideal situation for the student of nature, where also the contemplative mind would find its home. A Mr Hamilton who visited the Island during my stay on it as a watchman and who became a personal friend of mine, provided the following impressions:

> To the average person living in the midst of city life it seems hardly possible that there is an Island within the British Isles where there is no communication with the mainland, except during three months in the summer; yet this applies to the lone Isle of St Kilda. My first view of the Island after the ship had sailed through the sound of Harris, away out to sea some 50 miles distant in the Atlantic Ocean, a black speck could just be seen; after some 6 hours sailing, we arrived at the Island and anchored in Village Bay.
>
> In many cases it is almost impossible either for goods or passengers to be landed on the Island owing to the storms prevalent in these parts. I was fortunate, however, in arriving in comparatively calm weather and being able to land in the normal manner, namely by being rowed ashore in a ship's lifeboat to a small cement jetty on the Island itself. I might say however at

this time that this is by no means a normal procedure, as in a great many cases, it is impossible to effect a landing.

Strictly speaking St Kilda is not an Island but a miniature archipelago, although the name has been applied more particularly to Hirta, the Gaelic word meaning earth, the largest Island of the group, the circumference being approximately 10 miles and of a rough oval shape. The adjacent Islands being named Dun, Soay and Boreray, might be likened to the Bass Rock or Ailsa Craig with Stac Lee situated close by, a most peculiar rock formation, very similar to the pinnacle of a cathedral rising out of the water and which is a nesting place of thousands of gannets or solan geese. On climbing the cement steps of the jetty on Hirta, the first view that strikes the visitor is of a very small village situated around the foot of a colossal amphitheatre. It was on Hirta that the St Kildians made their homes and struggled for existence; the village now entirely deserted, consists of sixteen stone built cottages, each of three rooms, the roofs of which are tarred, and two larger houses and a small church.

The amphitheatre consists of a natural semi-circular mountain rising to a height of some 1,400 feet. One can readily appreciate the awesomeness and solitude of such a situation, with sixteen small cottages at the bottom of a mountain of this dimension. [At the time Mr Hamilton delivered this address, the Island belonged to the Earl of Dumfries and was used as a wild bird sanctuary.] Mr Gillies welcomed me on landing and expressed his great delight on seeing me; he having spent the previous three weeks on the Island by himself. I have now great pleasure in asking Mr Gillies to speak of his feelings during his lonely stay.

Mr Gillies

My feelings on seeing Mr Hamilton landing on the jetty were hardly to be described as my listeners may well understand; imagine being marooned somewhat like Robinson Crusoe.

Mr Hamilton

The weather during the period Mr Gillies and myself lived on the Island was, to put it mildly, very broken. The waves rising to terrific heights came crashing into the bay and, for myself at least, it was an unforgettable sight.

The first few days on the Island I devoted to exploring and it was during one of my walks that I had rather an alarming experience. As I have already explained, the hamlet, or village, lies at the foot of a mountain which is named Connacher. On ascending this mountain, which is 1,400 feet high, and which I may say is devoid of all trees or bushes or anything of a like nature, but which consists entirely of rocks covered with a shallow turf. In fact, up to the time of the evacuation two or three years ago, the natives of St Kilda had not seen a tree or a bush. Gillies and I plodded slowly up this mountain and I was longing to see the view from the summit but, on reaching that point, my heart nearly stopped. Imagine for one moment a mountain 1,400 ft high cut in half. That was what met my eye when I reached the top of Connacher. Directly below my feet was a cliff of 1,400 ft high sheer drop down to the sea. This was one of the most awful moments of my life. Had it not been for the presence of mind of Mr Gillies, I might not have been here to give this talk to you tonight. Looking down with my head over the edge of the cliff I could see waves of the Atlantic Ocean rolling in and breaking at the base of the cliff, but I could hear no sound owing to the great height. The birds, known as the fulmar and puffins, were flying about in their hundreds and appeared like midges in the air. On another occasion when I was descending a hill called Oiseval, situated to the north [*sic*] of Connacher, a very heavy mist came down without any warning and completely obliterated everything. On feeling my way down carefully, I found myself suddenly precipitated into empty space and on landing discovered I was up to the waist in a peat bog. I spent a very uncomfortable hour waiting for the mist to lift, which it did as suddenly as it descended, and I arrived at the house very wet and cold in time to meet Mr Gillies who was coming out to search for me. The feeling of utter loneliness is very great, especially when one does not know when one may be taken off the Island. I felt it very much after the first three or four days and I often wonder what the feelings of the natives were.

How did the loneliness react on the natives Mr Gillies?

MR GILLIES

The Islanders never felt lonely as they never knew any other home beyond St Kilda, and they had plenty to keep them occupied, during the winter month weaving the famous St Kilda tweed.

MR HAMILTON

What did the Islanders use for food?

MR GILLIES

We used to kill the sheep and salt them; also birds known as the fulmar, puffins and gannets. We used to sell the feathers and the fulmar oil and these commodities helped the natives to pay their rent for the croft and home.

MR HAMILTON

How many fulmars did the natives kill everyday?

MR GILLIES

Usually about 300 a day.

MR HAMILTON

And what methods did the St Kildian use to catch these birds?

MR GILLIES

We had a long bamboo stick with a wire loop attached to the end of it, something similar to that which a boy used for snaring trout, and the natives lowered themselves over the cliffs and killed the birds by casting the loop over their necks and choking them.

It is very interesting to have Mr Hamilton's experience on the lonely Island of St Kilda. Here are his own words and also as he felt:

MR HAMILTON

I just wish to give you a summary of my farewell to the loneliest Island on the British Isles: I may say that the [*word omitted*] calling for us had been unable to approach the Island for several days after the day appointed for departure, owing to the storms of the Atlantic. Mr Gillies and I were therefore reduced to very short rations. It is very difficult for me in such a talk as this to convey to you the terrible loneliness of St Kilda, and it was with perhaps joy mingled with regret that we saw the last of St Kilda hull down on the horizon.

On a long voyage most of us spend a lot of our time looking at the sea. Do we ever wonder how it came about that three quarters of the earth's surface is covered by salt water? It is hardly surprising that scientists differ in their views concerning the origin of the sea, so we will not venture any opinion beyond the safe guess that the earth must have been a very uncomfortable place during the sorting out process. It is believed that, except for comparatively minor encroachment or recession, the main features of the ocean are much the same as they were hundreds of millions of years ago. There are those who say the sea is increasing in volume and others say it is decreasing. We are however on more certain ground in considering that the sea is getting more salty. All over the world, rivers are washing minerals which are soluble and, as they become merged with the water of the sea, this gradually increases in density. I was always fascinated with the sea; and no wonder, as I would come out of our home on St Kilda, here the sea was staring at me. I was always interested watching wave after wave continuously dashing against the shores. Think too of the seaweed as small bits washed upon beaches but there are great jungles and forests of it with thousands of species, ranging from the smallest algae to ribbons of kelp, sometimes hundreds of feet in length. All this affords food and shelter for animal life and possesses valuable fertilising properties when strewn on the land, which was used by all the Islanders and found to be very productive.

Donald John Gillies Narrative Resumed

The year 1937, after ten years in Canada, round 1st May, the wife and I took our first sea voyage to the land of our birth. We boarded the passenger ship SS *Nova Scotia* in Sydney, Cape Breton, Nova Scotia. This particular ship sailed from Liverpool, England to New

York, Halifax and St John's Newfoundland. Calling at Sydney was a special occasion, taking on passengers on their way to attend the coronation of King George the Sixth. Left Sydney, Nova Scotia in the evening, bound for St John's Newfoundland, arrived St John's round noon on Sunday; a beautiful day. The wife and I attended divine service in the evening in St Andrews Presbyterian Church. After the church service we were entertained at the manse by the incumbent of the church. He drove us to the boat half an hour before it sailed and we had a glorious sea voyage. The sea was very calm all the way to Liverpool, England. We spent a week in Glasgow visiting relatives and friends and, after the week was up, the wife and I proceeded to Oban and took the SS *Lochinver*, one of MacBrayne's boats, over to Lochaline. We visited mother and the other members of the family in Larachbeg, Morven, and found them very happy in their new homes.

I did discover that they were very unhappy with their first home and of course there were legitimate reasons for that. The Ardness home was too small and quite a distance from school. As my brother John had a son at school age, the distance to school was considerable. The arrangement and the move to Larachbeg was ideal for school and also to quite a number of other St Kildian families. There was the MacKinnon family, my brother Donald and now mother, and the other natives of Larachbeg in that particular spot; it was very neighbourly indeed. So all in all I discovered that the St Kildians were very contented and happy working with the Forestry Department.

I took a picture of the group. The one with the beard was the oldest man that left the Island of St Kilda, Finlay Gillies. He was living at that time with his daughter Mrs Norman MacKinnon. Here was a man, as he said to me: I found myself in a similar situation as Jacob found himself when he stole his brother's birthright. He had to leave home and flee for his life. He left home not knowing where he was going and late evening he came to a brook, went into the brook and selected a few stones which became a pillow. He laid his head and had that magnificent dream of the ladder, bottom on earth and top in heaven, and angels ascending and descending on it. He woke up and said, 'This can be none other but the House of God and the very gate of heaven.' He related this instance to me. He continued saying, 'I did not know what the future had in store for me but I knew that God would provide for me', and he continued and quoted that verse of Scripture, 'Lo I'm with you and will never leave nor forsake you.' 'Donald, I put my trust in that promise and the Lord has never failed me and I'm certain He will not.' That same evening the group in the picture gathered in mother's residence and had worship and a social evening. One could not find any happier bunch anywhere than the St Kildians in Larachbeg and Savery in Morven. It was a pity for those that were sent to Tulliallan in Kincardine that a place could not have been found for them in Lochaline where they could visit one another and attend the same church as they were used to, as I believe that my Aunt, Mrs Neil Ferguson Senior, died of a broken heart.

I made an attempt, which failed, to visit St Kilda. On that occasion I took the *Claymore*, one of MacBrayne's boats to Lochmaddy, visited Tobermory, Coll, Tiree, Castlebay and Lochmaddy. I was to pick up the SS *Hebrides* at Lochmaddy on Monday as she was making a trip to St Kilda. I spent the weekend in Lochportan with a next door [neighbour] I had in St Kilda. He was a missionary, supplying the Church of Scotland mission. I spent a very enjoyable weekend and preached twice in Gaelic.

Monday morning joined the SS *Hebrides* in Lochmaddy. Unfortunately the captain came to me after he left Lochmaddy and I remember the words he used: 'Mr Gillies', he said, 'I hate to disappoint you but the weather is from the southeast and landing on St Kilda is impossible and I'm making for Tarbert.' So, instead of visiting St Kilda I visited St Kildians that left the Island before the evacuation of the Island, the family of the late William MacDonald who was our precentor on the Island for many years and a Godly man. He died at his daughter's residence in Uig, Lewis, so his widow had a home in Stornoway. I had a very nice and a pleasant visit. Her daughter Morag was at home when I arrived at the house. Mrs MacDonald was at church attending a communion service; however, she got a surprise to see me as I never sent word that I intended to visit Stornoway. This gracious woman was called home many years ago and I feel confident that she heard the Master saying, 'Well done good and faithful servant, thou wert faithful in few things, enter into the home that I have prepared for you from the foundation of the world.'

[*Returning to Canada*]

I returned from Stornoway to Larachbeg, from there to Liverpool and joined the sister ship of the SS *Nova Scotia*, the SS *Newfoundland* and landed in Halifax 1st July 1937. I returned to the manse at Indian Brook and served the congregation of North River and North Shore until 1939. On my return to the parish, I bought my second automobile, Chevrolet 1938. During my student days I did purchase a 1923 model T Ford. Those days you bought a car and then you applied for a licence and you received it, no car test or driving test. In May 1929 I was appointed as a student missionary to Marsboro, Quebec, so I had the car stored in a garage in Dunvegan, Ontario. When I served as a missionary during the summer of 1929, my first experience with the police as far as driving was concerned was returning with the car from Ontario to Quebec. I was in Montreal and I started out on the amber and a French policeman was standing on the corner so he pulled me aside and said, 'You went through a red light'. However I was silent. He asked for my licence and after showing it to him, he said, 'What's your occupation'? My answer was, 'A missionary of the Presbytery [*sic*] Church in Canada and I'm on my way to my summer missionary charge in Marsboro, Quebec.' He looked at me for a moment and then he said, 'Continue on your journey, preach Christ and Him crucified and mind the first red light you come to.'

The same day I arrived in Scotstown in the Eastern Townships. On my way to Marsboro two of my parishioners who were working in a saw-mill in this town, and as it was Saturday and knew that I was going to be passing their homes, asked for a ride. 'Gladly', I said. We were about 28 miles from Marsboro. On my way that late evening I came to a railway crossing and stopped as the law demanded. In front of me was a steep hill and coming down the hill was a car and he too stopped at the crossing, but hanging behind the back of his car was a French boy, and so he jumped off at the crossing right in front of my car, with the result that he fell to the ground. As a miracle would have happened, he went under my car at the front, passed over him and came out at the rear without a scratch but a little cut on his lip; so the French lad was lucky. That's the only two mishaps I had during my driving days and I drove until I was 80 so I did not renew my licence after that.

[*My Various Posts During and After World War Two*]

Second ocean voyage took place during the Second World War. I joined the army in 1942 in Sydney, Cape Breton, Nova Scotia. My first assignment was as chaplain to the Pictou Highlanders which served in the Newfoundland area. I returned from Newfoundland in 1943 and served in the Dartmouth area for a couple of months. I was posted to Portage La Prairie as a chaplain to paratroopers and served there for a short period of time.

From Winnipeg I was posted overseas, transferred from Winnipeg to Windsor, Nova Scotia. I boarded a troop ship in Halifax bound for overseas. We were the third last ship to go through the gates but we didn't continue too far until we noticed that we were returning to the Halifax harbour. The master of the vessel discovered that he had a defective compass, so that was the reason he returned and did not continue in that convoy. We were delayed for forty-eight hours and after that we joined a convoy that took us to Liverpool, England. I served for a couple of months as a chaplain in a hospital at Farnborough in England, crossed the channel to France in 1944, was chaplain with the 27th Canadian Regiment, was at Williams Haven at the Armistice and returned to Canada February 1946 aboard one of the Cunard Line and landed in

Halifax. I continued the journey by train to Winnipeg, Manitoba and met the wife in this city. After a few weeks in Manitoba, the wife and I made our first visit west which took us as far as Vancouver. The moment we saw this part of God's vineyard, we fell in love with it.

In April 1946 I was inducted into the pastoral charge of Vancouver Heights Presbyterian Church and remained in this charge until 1952. In October 1952 I resigned from this congregation and accepted the protestant chaplaincy in the British Columbia penitentiary, served in this capacity until I retired in the year 1966. I returned to church life again and accepted a call to Knox Presbyterian Church in Sooke on Vancouver Island. I only remained in this charge for three years and returned to Vancouver and accepted a part-time penology work with the Burnaby RCMP detachment. I resigned from this work in the year 1974.

[*Our Trip to Australia in 1974*]

In April 1974 the wife and I took our first big sea cruise on the P&O liner *Arcadia*, which took six weeks to make the journey from Vancouver, Canada, to Sydney, Australia, visiting Honolulu, Japan, Manila, Rabaul and then Sydney. Had a very pleasant trip; however, there is an instant that I should like to relate here. Arriving in Yokohama, Japan, four of us took a taxi to Tokyo. After arriving in Tokyo, the couple that was with us went in a different direction to us. Night came upon us and now time to return to the ship. We summoned a taxi but he could not speak a word of English and summoned the next one and experienced the same fate. Here we were stranded not knowing even the number of the pier the *Arcadia* was docked.

However, 'God works in a mysterious way, His wonders to perform'. Here was a young man standing not too far from us watching our performance and recognised that we were in real trouble. He tapped me on the shoulder and said, 'I think you are in trouble'. He spoke perfect English with the words 'can I help you?' He asked us where was the ship docked, here we could not even give him the number. So he went and phoned the police thinking that he could get a satisfactory answer. He came out of the telephone booth with the answer that the police were unable to give him the correct pier. Nevertheless he called a taxi and the three of us got in and made for Yokohama. He took us right to the ship.

I asked why he was there at that particular spot at that time; he was to meet a friend that did not show up. I asked this Japanese young man, 'Where did you learn your English?' The answer, 'From a Canadian professor'. We offered him remuneration which he refused. He said 'As you go along Life's highway you may come across someone in real need; help him regardless of his creed or nationality. This proves that the good Lord looks after His own.' The promise fulfilled, 'I will never leave thee nor forsake thee', which was proven to me that evening in Tokyo, Japan. That of course taught us a very valuable lesson; we never left the ship again without knowing the number of the pier our ship was docked at. We travelled in Australia, Melbourne. Here I met a St Kildian that went to school with me. Also I was greatly interested in the section of Melbourne called St Kilda. This name was given to this part of Melbourne by natives that left the Island of St Kilda many years ago, thirty families of them. [*The district was actually named after a ship called* The Lady of St Kilda – ed] Some of them returned to St Kilda for a visit. In 1928 a Rev. MacQueen from their part of Melbourne, his parents emigrated from the Island and made their home in that part of Melbourne called St Kilda.

Our visit to New Zealand was very pleasant; we found a lovely country with very hospitable people. On this occasion we visited with a St Kildian son, although this lad was born in Old Kilpatrick, his father was born in St Kilda and was my next door neighbour, Angus as he was called. He worked in the Old Kilpatrick shipyard for many years. He was a foreman in that shipyard and elder of the Kirk in the Church of Scotland in Old Kilpatrick. Angus MacDonald was well thought of by his fellow workers in the shipyard in Old Kilpatrick and also by the members of the Church;

he served faithfully and well. Angus paid a visit to Auckland a few years before he passed on to his eternal reward.

On this trip the wife and I visited North Island, New Zealand, a place called Waipu. The reason for this visit was to conduct divine service in St Andrews Presbyterian Church, an occasion we enjoyed immensely. This settlement once was a Scottish settlement, people that came from Assynt, Lewis, Harris and Uist. They first settled on Cape Breton Island, a place called St Ann's, from St Ann's they emigrated to that part of New Zealand called Waipu in the north land, a very attractive place. My first preaching station in Canada 1927 was in St Ann's and that's how I was introduced to Waipu in New Zealand by relatives back in Cape Breton, Nova Scotia. I returned to Vancouver on the P&O Liner *Oronsay* after spending a very pleasant and a very profitable holiday.

[*Our Trip on the Cruise in 1982 to the Holy Land*]

The cruise of 1982 round the world on the *Canberra* found this one to be most interesting from the educational point of view, and also spiritual. In my early teens I can recall father and morning devotion, reading in Gaelic the story of the Saviour's birth and also as the Saviour rose to manhood, His carpenter's shop, His trip to the lake of Galilee, calming the storm and walking on the sea. This story was very familiar to me, although on the Island Christmas was never celebrated. The Islanders didn't worry themselves as far as determining dates of birth, Crucifixion and Resurrection was concerned. Their belief was if the Bible said, that was enough and good enough for them. The highlight of the cruise was the visit to the Holy Land, my Sunday afternoon visit to Nazareth, and saw where Joseph, Mary and Jesus lived, a cave and also the carpenter's shop, the lake of Galilee, the feeding of the five thousand and also Cana and the first miracle performed by Jesus at the wedding feast turning the water into wine and Capernaum with its ruins of a second century AD synagogue.

A very attractive drive from Haifa was the drive to Jerusalem through the orange groves of the Sharon Valley. The first visit:

Mount of Olives, the traditional place of the Ascension, a sight that one cannot easily forget, the panoramic view of the city dominated by the Dome of the Rock. We descended down to the garden of Gethsemane and the adjoining church of all nations. After this we continued out to Bethlehem, where a visit was also made to the church of the nativity where in the grotto below the sanctuary a simple silver star set in marble marks the spot where Jesus was born. We saw the city wall and the palace of Pontius Pilate. I walked along the Via Dolorosa, the traditional way of sorrows along which our Lord walked carrying His cross and the visit to the Holy Sepulchre which contains the traditional sites of the Crucifixion, Burial and Resurrection. I also had the opportunity of visiting the Dome of the Rock and also visited several stations of the Cross. We were also shown the road to Emmaus. One has to keep in mind that during Christ's sojourn that the population was only four hundred [*sic*]. Today the population of Jerusalem is well over seventy thousand.

The tour medition [*sic*] as far as I was concerned was the following:

> In the beginning God created the heaven and the earth, and behold it was very good, Genesis 1: verses 1 and 31.
>
> In the beginning was the Word, and the Word was with God, and the Word was God. And the Word became flesh and dwelt among us full of grace and truth, John 1: verses 1 and 14.
>
> But while He thought on these things, behold the angel of the Lord appeared unto him in a dream saying, 'Joseph thou son of God [*sic*], fear not to take into thee Mary thy wife, for that which is conceived in her is of the Holy Spirit. And she shall bring forth a son, and thou shall call His name Jesus, for He shall save His people from their sins, Matthew 1: verses 20–21.

The birth of Christ is the sunrise of the Bible, even the centuries obey Him and swing there orbits around His cradle and date their calendar from His birth.

The Saviour comes!
No outward pomp
bespeaks his presence nigh,
No earthly beauty shines in Him
To draw the carnal eye, Paraphrases 25:2.

Where is He who has been born King of the Jews? We have come to worship Him, Matthew 2:2.

Let us go over to Bethlehem and see this thing that has happened which the Lord has made known to us, Luke 2:13.

When they saw the star they rejoined exceedingly with great joy and going into the house they saw the child with Mary, his móther and they fell down and worshipped Him. Then opening their treasures they offered Him, Matt 2:10–11.

And the shepherds returned, glorifying and praising God for all they had heard and seen, Luke 2:20.

It isn't far to Bethlehem town –
It is anywhere that Christ comes down
and finds in someone's shining face
A welcome and a biding place.
The road to Bethlehem runs right through
The homes of people like me and you. Anon.

This verse also struck as I stood at the tomb so I shall share it with you,

Christ by highest heaven adored,
Christ the everlasting Lord,
Late in time behold Him come,
Offspring of a Virgin's womb,
Veiled in flesh the Godhead see,
Hail the incarnate Deity,
Pleased as man with man to dwell,
Jesus our Immanuel.
Hark! the Herald angels sing,
'Glory to the newborn King'.

Indeed two days to remember, surrounded by the bare brown Judean hills, 28th and 29th March, I'm standing in the large courtyard of the Church of the Nativity in Bethlehem. From the outside the church looks more like a fortress and the courtyard is at the side of the white building. I enter the church by a low narrow doorway let into the blank wall. The reason for this small doorway is to make all who enter the church bend in reverence.

I'm in a lofty pillared hall. The pillars have been standing there since about AD 300 and are of beautiful pink marble. Straight ahead is the central altar; this belongs, mark you, to the Greek Church, and two black-clothed, black-bearded Greek priests are intoning passages from their Bible while another priest walks around them and the altar, swinging a censer.

At the left of this central altar is the altar of the Armenian Church. Two Armenian priests similarly dressed as the Greeks are finished. Thus the offering never ceases in this church. A third altar on the right belongs to the [*word omitted*]. On this Altar a large effigy of the Virgin Mary stands in a glass case and strewn on the floor of the case are many trinkets – rings, brooches, offerings of personal sacrifice from visiting pilgrims. I stood silently at the spot, birthplace of Christ.

In a recess hewn out of the solid stone and hung with red tapestry is the place of the birth. There is a large brazen star let into the floor. The vault is filled with large hanging brass lamps; some are said to be of gold and they are burning feebly. Down a few more steps is the manger similarly draped with red cloth.

I stood there, trying to cast my mind back across the centuries. As I stood there I noticed another party gathering quietly around the alcove with the star. I believe they sang a hymn. The sweet singing ends and one of their number offers a short prayer; each person knelt down and kisses the star. The party vanished and I stood alone and wonder. So the day came to a close and the coaches returned to Haifa following the same route as for the outward journey. We were served a very hearty lunch in St David

Hotel in Jerusalem. This ended one of the greatest tours in my life.

We left Haifa Monday 29th March, making for Greece, Athens. Our arriving time was 31st March and our stay was supposed to be twelve hours. On our arrival at Athens the weather conditions weren't favourable to land. As the launches were to be used, the captain decided that it was too risky to land passengers in Athens so he set the vessel on a course towards Naples. Naturally I was disappointed as I was prepared to explore some of the road that Apostle Paul discovered. I was geared to see Mars Hill as it is described in The Acts of the Apostles, chapter 17, verses 22–23, 'Then Paul stood in the midst of Mars Hill and said, Ye men of Athens, I perceive that in all things ye are too superstitious. For as I passed by, and beheld your devotions, I found an altar with this inscription, "To the unknown God" whom therefore ye ignorantly worship, Him declare I unto you'. I was looking forward to see this interesting Bible land but apparently it wasn't to be.

On account of missing Athens, it meant that we were in Naples, Italy, earlier than expected. We tied at the dock in Naples at 7 p.m. I would like to share with you some of my experience in Rome. From Naples to Rome the distance is approximately 300 miles. We had lunch in a very comfortable restaurant and after lunch we were taken to see the sights of Rome.

It was interesting to note as we passed along on the road to Salerno and Sorrento, these two names were well familiar during the Second World War. Driving via the Autostrada to Salerno, a stop was made at this historic town, the point where the allied troops landed in World War Two. The monastery [of Monte Cassino] that the Germans held so long but destroyed by allied bombers situated on a hill has now been rebuilt. Entering Rome, or as it is called the eternal city, we visited the Holy Steps and the Colosseum and the Monument to Victor Emmanuel the Second and the tomb of the Unknown Soldier. After lunch we visited the Basilica of St Peter, within the boundaries of the Vatican City. This is the largest place of worship in the world. One cannot describe the size of this building with all its statues, there are so many of them that one finds it impossible to start to name them.

One particular statue that took my great interest is one of St Peter. As I stood at this statue and observed the reaction of the crowd that was passing, some kissing the feet of the statue of St Peter, others would touch the feet with their hands and others I noticed stood in reverence before it, but my own reaction and thought as I stood and looked at it was this, the story that is found in the Gospel according to Luke chapter 22, the betrayal of Jesus, and especially from verse 54:

> Then took they Him and Led him and brought Him to the high priest's house and Peter followed afar off. And when they had kindled a fire in the midst of the hall and were set down together, Peter sat down among them. But a certain maid beheld him as he sat by the fire and earnestly looked upon him and said, This man was also with them [*sic*]. And he denied saying, Woman I know him not.

So the story goes on and the Lord turned and looked upon Peter and immediately Peter remembered and Peter went out and wept bitterly. My thoughts were on this portion of Scripture as I passed by St Peter's statue. It would take weeks to see what is to be seen in this great Basilica. So we arrived back at the *Canberra* at 10 p.m. at night and a beautiful supper was waiting for us in the Pacific Restaurant.

So the journey is about at end. Tomorrow morning we are landing in Southampton at 7 a.m., ending a world tour that was very interesting indeed and I'm thankful to my Lord that I was able to make such an historic tour.

[*Conclusion*]

Sitting beside me at the table is a lady that was in St Kilda eighty years ago. The conversation came about when there was a picture shown in the cinema entitled Puffin Come Home, and St Kilda was mentioned as one place that puffins nested in millions on the Island of St Kilda. So I asked her how did she enjoy her trip to this lonely Island, St Kilda. She is a native of Dunfermline. She didn't, she thought that the people were very rude talking their native tongue the Gaelic and they only could speak English. At that moment she wasn't aware that I was a native born of that Island; so my answer was, 'The same thing is happening on this cruise, when Germans meet, they speak German, when the Dutch meet, they speak Dutch'. So the Islanders were only speaking the mother's tongue which they loved, and I continued to enlighten this lady by saying some of them could not speak another language. But then however I told her I'm a native born of that Island and I love it. What a surprise it was to her. However I gave her one of the St Kildian books that I had; the paper cover by Tom Steele [*sic*]. I met another lady by the name of Janet MacLean, a native of Oban in Argyllshire. She visited St Kilda as a young girl and could not remember very much about it. Sixty years is a long time. In bringing this story to a close, I'm reminded of a story I heard a minister of the Church of Scotland using as an illustration in his sermon:

There was an elderly gentleman and he gathered around him on this special evening all his grandchildren: two boys and girl. 'Now', he said, 'I'm going to tell you a story, and listen', and of course nothing pleased those youngsters any better than hearing a story. He went on to say, 'I travelled the world and saw great sights. I have been in America, Australia, New Zealand, The Holy Land and Africa and many other places, but listen to this, I expect to see more wonderful places yet.' The youngsters were all ears, where was Granpa going next? He was silent for a moment, 'when I pass on from this world to the next. I wonder where will I be, what will be my surroundings and environments. I expect to see that beautiful land that is fairer than day and by faith we can see it afar'. And I place myself in the same category as the man that relayed that magnificent message which is as true today as the day it was spoken many many years ago.

Select Bibliography

Atkinson, Robert (1949) *Island Going*, Collins, London

Buchan, Alexander (1727) *A Description of St Kilda, the most remote Western Isle of Scotland*, Edinburgh

Connell, Robert (1887) *St Kilda and the St Kildians*, London

Ferguson, Calum (1995) *Hiort – Far na laigh a'ghrian*, Acair, Stornoway

Ferguson, Calum (2006) *St Kildan Heritage*, Acair, Stornoway

Fleming, Andrew (2005) St Kilda and the Wider World, Windgather Press, Cheshire

Flower, Robin (1978) *The Western Island or The Great Blasket*, Oxford University Press, Oxford

Harman, Mary (1997) *An Isle Called Hirte*, Maclean Press, Skye

Lawson, Bill (1993) *Croft History – Isle of St Kilda*, Bill Lawson Publications, Northton

Lawson, Bill (1993) *St Kilda and its Church*, Bill Lawson Publications, Northton

Lawson, Bill (2002) *Harris in History and Legend*, John Donald, Edinburgh

Lysaght, Patricia (2006) 'The Blasket Islands: Experience from Ireland', in *The Decline and Fall of St Kilda*, The Islands Book Trust, Lewis

MacDonald, Calum (forthcoming) *St Kilda – The Autobiography of a St Kildan*, The Islands Book Trust, Lewis

MacQueen, Calum (1995) *St Kilda Heritage*, edited by Kelman and Ewen MacQueen, Scottish Genealogy Society, Edinburgh

Martin, Martin (1698) *A Late Journey to St Kilda*, London

Meek, Donald (2007) ' "It Follows me, that Black Island . . . ": Portraying and Positioning the Hebridean 'Fringe' in Twentieth Century Gaelic Literature', in *Centring on the Peripheries: Studies in Scandinavian, Scottish, Gaelic, and Greenlandic Literature*, Norvik Press, Norwich

Quine, David (1988) *St Kilda Portraits*, Ambleside

Randall, John (2007) *St Kilda – Myth and Reality*, The Islands Book Trust, Lewis

Robson, Michael (2005) *St Kilda: Church, Visitors, and 'Natives'*, The Islands Book Trust, Lewis

Sands, John (1876 and 1878) 'Out of this World; or, Life in St Kilda', Edinburgh

Scottish Executive (2003) *Revised Nomination of St Kilda for inclusion in the World Heritage Site List*, Edinburgh

Steel, Tom (1965) *The Life and Death of St Kilda*, Glasgow